Audacious

Audacious

BETH MOORE

B&H
PUBLISHING GROUP

NASHVILLE, TENNESSEE

978-1-4336-9052-5

Published by B&H Publishing Group
Nashville, Tennessee

Dewey Decimal Classification: 248.843
Subject Heading: CHRISTIAN LIFE \ WOMEN

1 2 3 4 5 6 7 8 • 20 19 18 17 16 15

Contents

"Faith is not the clinging to a shrine

but an endless pilgrimage of the heart.

Audacious longing,

burning songs,

daring thoughts,

an impulse overwhelming the heart,

usurping the mind—

these are all a drive towards serving Him

who rings our hearts like a bell."

Abraham Joshua Heschel & Samuel H. Dresner in
I Asked for Wonder: A Spiritual Anthology

Acknowledgments

Twenty years of working with a publisher gives an author innumerable opportunities to say thank you. A writer doesn't stick around that long because she's miserable. She sticks around because, somehow amid the ink cartridges, e-mails, conference calls, texts, Skypes, manuscripts, deadlines, and edits, something clicked. Very different people from very different places and perspectives somehow landed on the same page and sent it to print. The whole process has never lost its wonder to me. God alone could forge the length, depth, and breadth of the ministry relationship I've had the privilege to share with LifeWay Christian Resources. That they are not sick to death of me by now is a wonder all its own so I will begin my thanks with them.

My beloved friends and colleagues at LifeWay, I would scour every dictionary in the English language if I could find a new way to say thank you for partnering with me in another message. Alas, I'm left with the same two worn-out words but I extend them with fresh affection and tremendous warmth. Faith, Paige, Amy, and Becky, I will remember for a very long time the conference call where we first discussed this project. In a planning meeting for the next calendar year, you let me spring this one on you for *this calendar year* and worked at lightning speed without any hemorrhage of excellence to get it done. That, my friends, is audacious. It could not be more fitting that this project required audacity on every level. Thank you for all the extra hours and extra effort. How I pray that you will never consider them wasted. Most of all, thank you for getting behind this message with such genuine passion. I will love you forever.

Jennifer Lyell, I loved every second of working with you. You are the best kind of editor: not too much, not too little. You're just right. I am so grateful for your feedback, both professional and personal. You worked hard and fast.

Keith Moore, not one manuscript in twenty years of writing would ever have been completed without your support. Being married to somebody as quirky as me is not for the meek or faint of heart. Thank you for not dropping your jaw and telling me I was out of my mind for adding this project into a busy schedule. To have a man who has continually said, "Baby, you can do this" is a gift of God beyond price. I love you furiously. Thank you for keeping me honest.

Amanda and Melissa, thank you for your company, your hilarity, your constant affection and your patience. If you don't buy what's in this book from this pen, it's worthless. No one on this earth means more to me than the two of you. No one on earth inspires me like you do. You are walking, talking manifestations of God's unfathomable grace to me. I love being your mother.

Curtis, my son-in-law and pastor, thank you for always praying for me and encouraging me and for continually being interested in what I'm working on. You are unspeakably dear to me.

Jackson and Annabeth, you delight me to no end and keep me forward-thinking in every artery of ministry entrusted to me. I cannot wait to see what Jesus will do with the two of you. I would not trade grandchildren with anybody on the planet. You have me.

GP, Susan, KMac, Kimberly, Jenn, Nancy, Sherry, Johnnie, Evangeline, Diane, and Mary, my co-laborers at *Living Proof Ministries* and dearest fellow sojourners: your hard work, your continual labors of love, your prayers, your encouragements, and your exhortations have enabled twenty years of books to be written that truly might never have otherwise landed on the page.

Travis, Angela, Christine, and Priscilla, you cheer me on tirelessly. You widen my world. You enlarge my heart. You make me laugh. You call me to believe. You stir me up. You make me brave.

Jesus, You light the stars, hang the moon, and set the sun ablaze. Your relentless love saved my life, saved my family, and saved my sanity. Any shred of dignity I possess is a testament to Your mercy. Be the driving desire of my life. Keep me.

A Vision Begging for an Adverb

I boarded a plane in Seattle under a spectacular cloudless sky to head back to my home on the outskirts of Houston. Mount Rainier was in a gratifyingly arrogant mood that day, wearing a heavy cloak of late-winter snow against a background of shocking blue. I had a bulkhead seat on the flight, meaning that I'd have to put my carry-on in the overhead compartment rather than having it handy under the seat in front of me. To occupy my time until I could get out of my seat and grab my laptop, I reached into my bag and pulled out a book my good friend, Travis, had passed on to me at our conference.

The second chapter of the book pitched out a set of simple questions—common ones really—that hit me with curious force like I'd never grappled with them before. *I had.* Most of us have. But, for me, it had been a good long time. People with a feverish student mentality tend to see everything through the lens of a classroom. I read a book and the author turns into a teacher and every question sends me back to a desk at Northbrook High, feeling a ridiculous obligation to answer. Trying to assemble my truest response to those two basic questions quaked my heart wide open somehow and compelled me to these pages. Nothing helps me hash things out like a blank Word document with a blinking cursor.

That night, just a few days ago as I write this, I tossed and turned, oscillating between sentences of a book I was already jotting in my head and a jillion sane reasons to put the whole idea to bed. *There's no time for this*, I kept telling myself. I had the next day off and spent it laughing, musing, and eating with my two adult daughters by a crackling fire on my back porch in the woods. No one can get my mind off work like they can. Their company is a Sabbath to me. Their lively conversation, pure inspiration.

We three can work through subjects at warp speed and adapt to each one with a brand new mood. The harder the season we're going through, the funnier we tend to get to each other. It's not that we like to be miserable. It's that we share a deep-abiding commitment to milking the absurdity out of every *holy cow* of a calamity that treats itself to the grass in our pastures. We cry hard. We laugh hard. So when my girls are with me, I'm with them. That evening I shoved aside the surging in my soul and gave full sway to my world's favorite company but, as their cars backed out of the driveway, that compelling pulled right back up, parked itself in my chest and revved cantankerously.

So today I write. Maybe I'll talk myself out of this by tomorrow but today I write.

Maybe this is a fitting time to say that, as much as anyone you will ever meet, I believe that God can use a book to mark a life. It doesn't even have to be a great book. It can just be well-timed. He can cause a set of pages to hit a pair of hands with the kind of timing that sparks a decision that marks a destiny. Something within those pages becomes a catalyst that shapes a calling. I believe this to my bones not because I am an author but because I am a fellow reader and lover of books. Several years ago, I wrote these words as part of the introduction to a Bible study:

> *In the beginning stages of writing this series, a dimension of my life became so hard and had gone on for so long that I felt I could no longer bear it. I wanted to quit in the worst way. In the midst of it, I read a book. It doesn't matter which one it was because God can use anything He wants. I bawled at the end of it. Bawled till the tears were dripping off my nose and into my lap. Bawled until my lungs felt fluish and hot. The book talked about having the courage to live under strain and pain to be part of a better story. A larger story. It said not to wimp out. That only pain can bring about change. And, as a writer, not to be satisfied with writing a life I'm not willing to live. You're wondering what's new about that. But, then again, you know better than that. A subject doesn't have to be new. It just has to speak to the predicament you're in right now.*[1]

But it doesn't have to be a predicament, although who on God's green earth doesn't have one? The timing could, instead, be about a longing you can't seem to fill or a dullness you can't seem to shake, or a purpose you can't seem to find or a passion you can't seem to keep. You don't even need to know you *need* a thing for God to *use* a thing. You just read, perhaps, for the felicity of well-arranged words or out of severe allergy to boredom. Those were two of my reasons several days ago on the plane when I pulled that book out of my carry-on and threw it in my seat.

---

1. *James: Mercy Triumphs* (Nashville: LifeWay Christian Resources, 2011), 9.

The name of the book was *21 Great Leaders: Learn Their Lessons, Improve Your Influence* authored by Pat Williams, a motivational speaker and senior vice president of the NBA's Orlando Magic. Several pages in, it was just me, God, and a good book—and all the surrounding chatter folded into a wormhole of white noise. I'd already underlined several sentences and scribbled notes in a few margins when I got to the middle of page thirty-five and took pause at two questions:

What is your dream?
What is your vision for the future?

The brief paragraph ended with Williams's challenge to the reader: *Write down your vision. Post it on the wall. Read it every day.*

I can't think of a time in several decades that those two questions would have been more relevant to me. One week before I read the book, I'd flown with my whole beloved family to Nashville to celebrate and commemorate twenty years of Bible study ministry with a publishing group that had long-since become like family to me. We'd spent the better part of two days together in small groups and large, acknowledging the astonishing grace and faithfulness of God and reminiscing about all the wild things we'd experienced. In the midst of incredibly hard work, woefully long hours, and back-breaking tapings over the course of two decades, we'd also managed to eat pizza on the top of the Mount of Olives, ride motorcycles on the Island of Patmos, stand ankle-deep in sheep manure in Bethlehem, and celebrate Purim on raucous streets of the old Jerusalem with little girls dressed up like queens.

A small team of us had also hauled a replica of the Ark of the Covenant all over the Utah desert trying to capture a perfect silhouette of priests in the wilderness for a series opener on the Old Testament tabernacle. We were reduced to one camera because four of the men on the film crew were required to stand in as the priests carrying it. They did so wearing terry cloth bathrobes over their shorts and flip-flops on their huge hairy feet to feign ancient sandals. Clearly not one of those men had ever had a pedicure. One was such an avid runner that what few toenails he had left were black. In the great oratory tradition of Emilio in the movie *Mr. Deeds*, the hideousness of those feet will haunt my dreams forever. These were the kinds of things we'd recounted as we'd commemorated twenty years. These and the innumerable graces of God. For me, it had been an unprecedented time of looking back.

None of us had the feeling that our journey together was over or that God's purpose for our converging paths had come to an end. The best kinds of commemorations are when you're not saying good-bye and, God willing, we weren't—but, having officially waved at the past, we could either turn to the future or turn in our resignations. It seemed a tad early for that so we left the celebration bidding one another face-forward, whatever God might bring. And, so, a few days later, there on the page of that meddling book was this:

What is your dream?
What is your vision for the future?

Those two questions wouldn't have even given me pause six months earlier but, suspended there in midair on that plane between my past and my future, suddenly they flew their way back into play like a pair of homing pigeons. I leaned my head back against the headrest, stared into space from way up high and let the questions sink way down low like weighted hooks into a sea. I wanted them to fish up something true. Something at the very bottom. You may as well go ahead and start thinking about what you'd fish up from that ocean floor because I'm going to ask those same questions of you before this book is over. I'd had one mission statement embroidered into the fabric of my soul for years and could say it in my sleep: to see women come to know and love Jesus Christ. It had not wavered for thirty seconds in three decades. Every Bible study, book, CD, and DVD on our ministry shelves and every download on our website was a shot at that goal.

So, the question on the tray table was this: do I still have the same personal vision? Nothing would be wrong with that. What's not to like about a proverbial long obedience in the same direction? *If that's it,* I told myself, *just go ahead and own it.*

So I flipped to the blank space on the inside of the back cover to do just what the author told me to do: *Write down your vision.* At first I couldn't get my pen to commit to the page. I made at least fifteen false starts. If you're the compulsive sort, you understand. For one thing, I wished my handwriting were better. After all, what if I ever wanted to take a picture of it with my cell phone and make it my screen saver? Or what if I wanted to get a banner made out of it at Kinkos to hang on the outside of our office building? I didn't want to but, I'm just saying, what if I did? Or what if I loaned someone the book and she turned to the back and saw it and was disgusted with my penmanship? Don't tell me that can't change the way you feel about a person. You like a person, respect a person, make certain assumptions about a person, and then you see her sign her credit card receipt at the end of lunch and she has the handwriting of a psychopath. There's no going back.

The second hang-up was even more neurotic: I was prepared to give myself only one shot at it. For some inexplicable reason, I felt like I had to word it right the first time. The safest thing I could do was simply write the exact same mission statement as my ongoing vision: *To see women come to know and love Jesus Christ.*

But I couldn't make myself do it. I'd seen too much in the last several decades to leave well enough alone. I'd traveled too far, talked to too many people and heard too many stories. I'd been through too much. I was no longer new to this thing, no longer remotely as naïve, and no longer satisfied to leave the vision there.

I wanted more for women than that. I wanted them to come completely alive. I wanted them to find out what they were doing here and do it. I wanted them to tumble headlong into something vastly more influential over their futures than their pasts. Something so enthralling that they couldn't quit. Something they wouldn't miss for the world. Something too big for them to hide.

I wanted the same thing for them that I wanted for myself. Something that would require audacity. After twisting my intestines into a pretzel to sort it all out, I decided with considerable relief that what I wanted as a vision for the rest of my labors wouldn't take scrapping my original statement. It would just take tweaking. The sentence needed two words: one tiny little adjective and one lively adverb.

This book is about that adverb begging to carve a place so I'm making way and giving it space first:

Audaciously
ᐯ
To see women come to know and love Jesus Christ.

For two reasons:

Because He's worth it. Many years into this thing, I haven't lost interest, calmed down, or found that a life of fiery faith wasn't all it was cracked up to be. As it turns out, Jesus is bigger than I thought, better than He'd seemed, and more willing and able than I'd believed. In a human experience fraught with disenchantment and disappointment, I have thus far found no end to the pure thrill of Him.

The second reason is why you're holding this book. Because I am convinced to the last particle in me that, there in that audacious love, you will find the life you were born to live.

About That Tiny Little Adjective

O ne more little word is aching to inch its way into a fresh version of a thirty-year vision. It throws the whole thing over the edge, but I am convinced with every sane thought in my head that it's the blood-pumping heart of the gospel. That one tiny adjective is *all*.

*To see all women come to know and **audaciously** love Jesus Christ.*

It's an unreasonable, illogical, and unreachable vision. Many may not, but all *can*. Jesus came here for all. He gave His life for all.[1] In the wording of 1 Timothy 2:6, He gave His life as "a ransom for all." Titus 2:11 puts a megaphone to the mouth of the gospel with enough volume

---

1. 2 Cor. 5:14

to reverberate over the entire globe: "For the grace of God has appeared with salvation for all people."

All people.

He won't force it on you but it is yours if you want it. It is yours if you want Jesus.

And here's the thing. I think you do. You may not know it yet but He is and He has what you are aching for. No matter who you are, where you've been, what country, what religion, or lifestyle you're in, the life you were born to live is wrapped up in Him. That claim takes some kind of audacity to make, I know. But that's what these pages are all about. Audacious love. His for you. Yours for Him. That's what unleashes the life you're longing for. I'm not talking about just getting in the door. I'm talking about getting out there on the dance floor. You may not think you're the dancing type but maybe you haven't heard the music yet.

My hope in this chapter is to take ten quick minutes to address with esteem a reader who may be resistant to the whole Jesus element. I'd like to be straightforward with you and ask you to be willing to hear me out in these next few pages. If you find them tolerable, then maybe you'll consider sticking with the book to the end. It's a quick read so you don't have much to lose. If you're like me, you're itching to move on to another book about midway through the one you're reading anyway. My hope is that, by the time you're getting antsy, you'll have reached the last page.

I don't even care if you read it just to criticize it. I'm just asking you to consider it one woman's take on the human experience and the capacity to feel most alive based on a bit of living, searching, studying, trying, testing, and observing. If we were sitting across the table from one another, I'd let my coffee get cold to hear the same thing from you. What people think life is all about intrigues me and gets me thinking even if I don't agree with them. And I don't mind thinking. I hope you don't either.

I hope to throw out a challenge to you that God has used to keep me fully engaged and enthralled in this relationship with Him for decades on end and not just me. Because of the nature of my work, I stumbled into a lifelong case study of what makes females tick. You might be amused to know that this case study started in an advanced aerobics class I began teaching at twenty-two. If you don't think you can learn anything from a bunch of women in leotards, you missed the eighties. Stomach crunches have a way of bringing out what a woman's made of. If she's ever going to cuss, it's going to be somewhere right around minute four. So you keep the music good and loud. It's a mercy.

Over time, the kinds of classes changed and, since it was a bit unseemly to teach a Bible course in a leotard, I traded my Reeboks for spiked heels and hit the road. Along that perilous and beautiful way, I have had the incredible privilege of meeting, studying, and interacting with more women than I have the math skills to count. I developed a long-term fascination with what seems to keep a fire blazing in the hearts of some, while others of similar basic beliefs struggle along with a flicker. They get bursts of heat here and there but soon relapse into a frustrating malaise, even in the midst of doing good things and trying to live beneficial lives. Their eternal destiny is in order but maybe they'd pictured that life this side of it was going to be really different, too. They thought it would be motivating and meaningful in a way that lasted for more than thirty minutes at a time. Why wasn't it? Difficulty is a common denominator for everyone, so the key is not ease, nor does it appear to be finances, or even career choices. I'm not even sure the difference is dominated by health.

Take Mary Olive, for instance. I met her at a Starbucks several years ago where I'd planted myself in the sunshine at an outside table to do some writing. She rolled up right next to me in a wheelchair with an oxygen tank attached to the back of it. She was in her eighties but her eyes sparkled with a youthfulness I can't shake from my memory. She'd been a missionary in South America for decades but failing health had forced her home to the States. There she was, stuck in a chair, dependent on tubes for air, and, as she spoke, a torch emanated from her soul that could have melted a glacier. Something about her was breathtakingly beautiful. A sixteen-year-old could have walked past me in a pair of shorts with perfect legs and, if someone had asked me that very moment which girl I'd rather be, I'd have jumped in the body of that woman in the wheelchair in one second flat. I pulled out of that parking lot an hour later completely riveted and surer than I had ever been.

From my experience and observation, one match can light up our affections and keep them ablaze for as long as we're willing to keep that stick in the fire. I'm talking about the full stretch of a lifetime, through incredible stresses and upsets and gains and losses. Through countless disappointments in people and in ourselves. That one match would light the heart of anyone anywhere, male or female, and keep it burning. Through the pages of this book, we're giving that match a name: *audacity*.

If it's Christians you don't like, I get it. I don't like a few of them either. But I'm asking that you not confuse them—or me, or any other flesh and blood—with Jesus. He is in a class all by Himself. Call me crazy but, for the life of me, I can't find a lot not to like about Him. Who else in the entire human experience is incapable of doing you wrong or leaving you stranded or betraying your trust or wasting your time? Who else never recoils at the sight of the real us? Or gets bored with us? Who else never makes a promise He doesn't have the power to keep? Who else can perform a wonder in a wasteland?

Our perception of Jesus is sketched on the canvas in pencil swayed strongly by this point of view: do we see Him as a giver or a taker? Naturally, the only healthy inclination is to flee from a taker and run to a giver. It's not that Jesus has never taken anything from me because He has. He's taken shame from me, frequent defeat, paralyzing fear, debilitating guilt, and chronic regret. Well, and jealousy. There was that. And a ton of insecurity. That's not to say we don't lay some things down and make some sacrifices on the path of following Jesus. We do, but as they say, therein lies the paradox. Self-importance turns out to be self-sabotage and getting over ourselves turns into finding ourselves. Our true selves. The lives we were born to live. We'll never catch a glimpse of vision with our eyes rolled back in our heads. We'll slit the throat of our own satisfaction with the silky smooth feather of self-focus. Jesus worded it this way in Matthew 10:39:

"Anyone finding his life will lose it, and anyone losing his life because of Me will find it."

Those willing to give up their insatiable self-preoccupation to identify with Jesus and follow Him furiously will find an ever-unfolding life and love that they couldn't have scripted if they'd tried. *We all, with unveiled faces,* 2 Corinthians 3:18 says, *are looking as in a mirror at the glory of the Lord and are being transformed into the same image from glory to glory.* Another translation says it this way: *from one degree of glory to another.*[2] God knew better than to lay it all out there at once. With brilliant mastery,

---

2. ESV

He insisted on mystery. We don't get an advance bio of the precise life we're trading our self-absorption for. Even that is a gift from the giver. God authored a masterpiece of a story by setting into motion a process that would require a journey of faith. It was meant to be a nail-biter. It was intended all along to be a process that would require the naked exposure of our most sacred, carefully-guarded human possession: our trust.

For some of you, that's the deal breaker. That's the one thing you're not willing to fully expose and invest. The relational last frontier. I understand that in every way. In my most fundamental childhood years, the person I needed to trust the most was the person I could trust the least. When protectors turn into perpetrators, nothing comes harder for us. But I believe that inherent in the human journey is the lifelong search for someone worthy of our trust.

We get brave enough to throw it out there then, when the person turns out to be equally human, we withdraw and withhold—and, over time, the dreamer in us starts to wither and lose hope. I don't mean the daydreamer or the fairy chaser who refuses to get a grip on reality and grow up. I'm talking about that part of us that possesses the capacity our Creator tucked into every human soul for childlike faith. Not childlike behavior, childlike emotion, or childlike naiveté and gullibility. At some point a person ought to have to give up the pull-ups and quit sucking life out of a sippy cup. What Jesus talked about was childlike *faith*. The belief that someone out there is all he's cracked up to be. That something exists beyond what eyes can see.

There is a dreamer somewhere in all of us who wants to believe in ridiculous things like happy endings, enduring romances, quests and kingdoms, buried treasures worth hunting, and valiant adventures worth sweating and bleeding for. We have a dreamer in there who wants to believe that good really can overcome evil and that, one glorious day, the poorest of the poor will be the richest of the rich.[3] I'm talking about the kind of dreamer that believes every life has an actual purpose and that a plan is in motion that can and will and must turn out well. The Bible shamelessly validates every single one of those dreams with a corresponding reality.

The Maker of heaven and earth embedded deep within the human psyche an innate suspicion that He is out there. We can silence it, of course, but it takes a fair amount of commitment to keep it silent. More often it whispers in the quiet when we're all alone and squirms in the stillness when we've got no place to go. The writer of Ecclesiastes called it "eternity set in our hearts." When we're courageous enough to sit in the dark without the light of a cell phone, we know instinctively this life can't be it. We know that our physical bodies seem ill-fit for our ageless souls.

Though death and dying are as natural as birth and living, we are insulted and offended by them with the vehemence of a creature designed to outlast them. Animals don't resist death like humans do. Something in us keeps on insisting that dying seems wrong, like we're malformed for it. Maladjusted to it, even after innumerable generations of sons and daughters who can't, for the life of us in all our evolving, find a way to avoid it. We've never really believed that seeing is believing. We stare at the sea wondering about the deep. We stare at the stars wondering how far we are from a whole different world.

If we have not beaten the living daylights out of that dreamer within us, we know somewhere deep inside of us that God is out there, that He can be found and known, and that perhaps the person we were created to be is found and known in Him. We may not want to want Him. But we do. We were fashioned to. We are dying to find someone worthy of our unabashed, wholly unguarded trust. We're all looking for Jesus. We just

---

3. James 2:5

15

keep looking for Him in other faces, palms, and places. When we do find Him, we find the Giver.[4] That part of us dying to find someone to freely give ourselves to was created in His image.

Nothing Jesus will ever woo us to lay down on His behalf is worth what we'd miss if we didn't. If He wants your hands free, He has something to put in them. If He wants your feet loose, He has somewhere to plant them. If He wants your mouth shut, He has a new set of words to put in it. He's not trying to cheat you or trick you. He's not placing bets on you or playing games with you. He does not dispense grace with an eyedropper. He drenches us with it. He does not offer bare existence. He extends life abounding in blessing, power, passion, and purpose. If people told you God was stingy, they didn't know their Bible.

There's this fabulous scene in the Gospel of John where Jesus sends His disciples to town to grab some lunch and He stays behind and meets a woman at a well. She'd been preoccupied for years, repeating the same relational cycle, filling up the same empty jar the same empty way, looking for the life she was longing for. We're not told her name. It's easier that way to give her ours. She had no idea that audacious love was staring her right in the face. He said four words to her that I think He wants to say to each of us:

"If you only knew."[5]

You. Not someone else you know. Not someone needier. Not someone less self-sufficient. Not someone gutsier. Not someone more religious.

---

4. Rom. 8:32
5. John 4:10a NLT

Once the woman knew, she left that jar, ran into town and told everybody she could find to come and see. Because, once you know, you want everybody else to know, too.

> *"If you only knew the gift God has for you*
> *and who you are speaking to, you would ask me . . ."*[6]

That's what Jesus said. If you only knew what He has for you. Not only after you kiss this life good-bye but, here on this earth and now in this season. If only you knew, your heart would be so swept up in audacious love that nothing could keep you from the life you were born to live.

You can forget about not being His type. I did a little research in the New Testament from the first page to the last and drew up a list of every female on sacred record who was personally impacted by Jesus. The age-span stretched the slack out of a tape measure all the way from a little girl to a woman in her eighties. Some among them were single; others married, widowed, and divorced. Some were impoverished; others were wealthy. Some were just getting by and some were of means enough to support Jesus and His band of disciples on the traveling circuit.[7] Some of the women marked by Jesus were moms and some were not. Some were in ministry; others were merchants. Some were religious types. Still others, not. They were just like us.

In Acts 16, a very successful businesswoman is just one verse removed from a girl enslaved and trafficked.[8] Among the women who encountered Christ in the pages of Scripture, you find the devastated,

---

6. John 4:10 NLT
7. Luke 8:3
8. Acts 16:14–16

bleeding, busy, grieving, sick, dying, doubting, thriving, adulterous, ambitious, wise, despised, demon-possessed, and severely oppressed. So, if you are drawing breath, you're Christ's type. If Mary Magdalene couldn't run Him off with seven demons, you're probably out of luck.

He has come looking for you. And somewhere deep inside of you is a girl looking for Him.

Do You Love Me?

You're in a restaurant sitting at a table with a handful of your coworkers. You have all ordered the same thing. It is the special of the day: charcoal-grilled fish—fresh, not frozen—and bread so warm from the oven that a cloud of steam escaped as you broke open the crust. You didn't realize how hungry you were until the plate was in front of you. You'd worked all night. You knew you weren't going to sleep anyway. Too much anxiety. The last couple of weeks had been incredibly stressful. The ups and downs were outrageous, like a heart monitor topping and bottoming out, beeping frantically in a system overload. Highs that seemed sure to last suddenly free-fell into lows so dark and deep that they could find no floor. As if it all hadn't been tragic enough, you'd made a string of serious mistakes and miscalls and everybody at the table knew it. No one said much. Your coworkers knew that, had it not been you, it could have been them.

Then, the upshot came with such force, your spine whiplashed like a thin rope in the hand of a thrashing giant. Of course you were glad. Well, more than glad. You were ecstatic. Relieved. But still shaken. After the unexpected place the whole thing had gone, where was it going from here? Trauma and triumph were tangling inside of you, scrapping for the same space. Your nerves were shot. Your mind was stunned. Your heart was sore.

You needed this meal.

This break.

This group of people around this table. No one else could understand.

Then he—the head of the whole thing, the one you'd signed up for, the most magnetic and powerful man you'd ever met, the one you'd idolized and left everything for—leans across the table toward you, locks eyes with you, addresses you by your whole name then follows it with these words:

"Do you love me?"

Your answer is automatic. You make it quick. *"Yes, Sir, you know I do."*

He sets his elbows on the table and leans a little further in and then he says your name again so there's no mistaking who he's addressing. You don't know how much to read into the fact that he's not calling you by your nickname. He'd given it to you himself so he hadn't likely forgotten it. You wonder, after the way you dropped the ball, if he'll ever call you that again. You look up at him nervously hoping he's moved on to the coworker sitting beside you but he hasn't. You fidget in your chair. That's when he poses the question a second time.

"Do you love me?"

You're baffled, unsure of what he's after. You rub your bottom lip with your index finger and glance right and left. You can feel the heat in your face. That last bite of fish you'd eaten threatens to swim back up your throat. You swallow hard, take a deep breath, and answer the man again. *"You know that I love you."*

He pauses just a moment but his gaze never shifts. His hands stretch out on the table, his fingers slide wide apart, and his shoulders move further forward. He squints, his brows drawn down, like he's looking straight through your brain to the back of your skull. Then he speaks your name a third time. You've had a hundred conversations with him over the course of three years but you've never once heard him sound exactly like this. You can't quite characterize how he's coming across. The tone of his voice isn't accusing, really, but it's alarmingly intense. Then here it comes again like an umpire on the edge of *three-strikes-and-you're-out.*

"Do you love me?"

You feel sick. Singled out. Whatever this is, it's personal. Grief ties a knot in your throat and thickens your lungs. Your response begins with this: "You know everything." You didn't say it to flatter him. You said it because it's true. You've never met anyone like him in your entire life. He can read a mind and test a heart like nobody else on earth. Does he see something in you that you can't? Does he know something about you that you don't? Is there something he wants for you that you won't?

Everything in you begs to ask him the exact same question he keeps asking you. But you don't. You don't because you know the answer. You know he does. You even know that he did when you did what you did. Those deep brown eyes piercing your soul from across the table are not fixed on your face because he's unfeeling. They're fixed on your face because he's unfailing.

You would later know the questions were for your good and not your harm. They'd scroll across the screen of your thoughts at times of greatest consequence. They'd lodge a word in your vocabulary that you couldn't have written without. They'd become iron in your blood when you felt weak and fire in your bones when the glacial climb got steep. You'd one day realize that those very questions gave you the chance to say what you'd been born to say.

But that would come later.

This is now. You drop your hands into your lap and squeeze your eyes shut. You then open them, lift your chin, look straight at him and speak. *"You know that I love you."*

The scene is painful to imagine from the seat of that chair. Embarrassing, really. But if it were Jesus sitting straight across from you at that table and He'd loved you and chosen you before time began and assigned you a future with everlasting impact, you'd just have had the most vital dialogue of your believing life.

Throw back the calendar several thousand years and shift the scene from a restaurant to a shore in Galilee. Look for smoke coming from a charcoal fire and the bones of grilled fish picked white and clean. Don't bother looking long for any leftover bread. The only stray crumbs would probably turn up in a crusty fisherman's beard. Find Jesus in the scene first. He's both host and cook. Then study the other men until you find the one whose hair is damp. That will be the guy who threw on his robe, dove from the boat, and swam like a madman in the nippy waters of early Spring.

A man had shouted from the shore, "Men, you don't have any fish, do you?"

That's just the question a boatload of professional fishermen vies to hear. Then the man, a carpenter by family trade nonetheless, commences to tell them how to do their jobs. Don't lose sight of that little detail because the conversation one of them will have with Him is meant to have an inseparable connection to the job he'll be assigned.

"Cast the net on the right side of the boat," He told them, "and you'll find some." So they did, and they were unable to haul it in because of the large number of fish. (John 21:6)

There are know-it-alls that only *think* they know it all and then there's a know-it-all that really does know it all. The catch that nearly sunk the boat conveyed that they'd come into contact with the latter. This is the point in the scene when one of the fishermen on board, the ablest to see the shore with the youngest set of eyes, says to the one named Simon Peter, "It is the Lord!"

And Simon Peter? He up and jumps overboard. I love how Scripture words it. He *plunged into the sea.*[1] Hence, the wet head.

The rest of the guys get *out on land*, we're told, and Jesus invites them over to the charcoal fire where He's grilling fish and baking bread. This is the precise place our opening scenario originates. Read it for yourself in John 21:15–17:

When they had eaten breakfast, Jesus asked Simon Peter, "Simon, son of John, do you love Me more than these?"

"Yes, Lord," he said to Him, "You know that I love You."

"Feed My lambs," He told him.

1. John 21:7

A second time He asked him, "Simon, son of John, do you love Me?"

"Yes, Lord," he said to Him, "You know that I love You."

"Shepherd My sheep," He told him.

He asked him the third time, "Simon, son of John, do you love Me?"

Peter was grieved that He asked him the third time, "Do you love Me?" He said, "Lord, You know everything! You know that I love You."

"Feed My sheep," Jesus said.

Not *Do you believe Me?* Not *Do you admire Me?* Not *Do you appreciate Me?* Not *Do you worship Me?* Not *Do you respect Me?* All those questions have profound placement in the life of faith but they are not synonymous with the one Jesus deliberately, repeatedly asked Peter. The question was, *Do you love Me?*

With every ounce of conviction in my soul, I believe Jesus brought you and me to each side of these pages to ask us the exact same question. "_____ (imagine or write your name in that blank), *Do you love Me?*"

And I don't think He wants to ask us once. I think He means to lean in and keep asking it, just like He did with Peter, until we move past our automatic answer into the place of searching, squinting, and squirming. The second question sends us from the automatic gear to the assessment mode. Here, we're not only trying to figure out how to answer. We're trying to figure out what the inquirer is after. Then the third time around either makes us defensive, mad, frustrated, or sad but, if we cooperate, it plunges us down there into the tender quick where our authentic answer resides.

Here's the beauty of it: not one word of the divine inquisition is for sake of judgment or condemnation. Not one iota for the purpose of provoking guilt. Not one whit to expose failure or weakness. Not one syllable to embarrass us in front of our peers. In fact, the most fabulous thing that could happen for some of us in this chapter is to come to the shocking, wide-eyed realization that, truth be told, our answer would be *no*. If your answer way down there in the tender quick is *yes*, stick with it and don't let anybody talk you out of it. But, if in that hidden place, some of us realize that our most honest response is probably *no*, then take a deep breath and exhale the carbon dioxide of sheer relief.

At least then we could get on with it and open ourselves to the real thing. But, as it is, sometimes we just keep going on and on with this gnawing sense in our soul that something is missing but, because we assumed that what we felt was love, it slips through our fingers like a palm-full of parched sand. We know this whole following-Jesus-thing is not turning out as soul-riveting as we were promised but we certainly don't feel like we can divulge our disappointment to anyone. It would be sacrilegious, wouldn't it, or, at the very least, superficial? So, we just keep dragging our heels forward guessing that the sacrifice itself is meant to be the reward. And a horrible question haunts us in the night.

Is this all there is to it?

No. It's not. Jesus ties up the three-question divine inquiry with two words to Simon Peter: "*Follow Me!*" (John 21:19). Following Jesus is meant to be driven and drawn by love. Audacious love.

The easy confusion comes from mistaking a host of other really wonderful things for love.

I respect Jesus.

I deeply appreciate Jesus.

I believe in Jesus.

I serve Jesus.

So surely I love Jesus. Right? Those are extravagant verbs with vital places in our excursion with Jesus but they're not equivalents to love. They stand together in a lineup but one is taller than the rest so the others can grow in its strength. When a scribe asked Jesus in Mark 12:28 which of all God's commandments was paramount, He reached into the warm, beating heart of the law and raised these words above the rest:

"This is the most important . . . Love the Lord your God with all your heart, with all your soul, with all your mind, and with all your strength."[2]

Only love actually qualifies as love.

And love carries a feeling. Not every second of every minute, of course, but it has frequent enough feeling involved in it to characterize the whole attachment. Is that fair enough? We know this instinctively with every other relationship in the human experience. Set aside all the times we toss around the word *love* to convey how we feel about a movie or a meal and let's limit it to the real thing.

If I ask you which of your friends you really like and which of your friends you truly love, you'd answer the latter with the names of those who draw the deepest affections from you. If you're a mom and I ask you to describe your love for your children, your response would be incomplete without references to the feelings and emotions they stir up in you. Let's switch sides at the table and have you ask me a question.

How about this one: "Beth, do you love your husband?"

---

2. Mark 12:29–30

You'd want to punch me if I launched headlong into, "Of course I do! I cook for him every single day, I iron his shirts, gas up his car, drive right behind him in mine, and I do every single thing he tells me to do."

Wouldn't you want to say, "I didn't ask you if you work hard for your husband. I asked you if you loved him." By the third time you pushed me for an answer, I'd start getting a clue what you were after. You want to know if I could get tears in my eyes at the remotest thought of ever having to live without him. You want to know if something still happens in my heart when I get a glimpse of him waiting for me at a table for two in an Italian restaurant. You want to know if he and I still slow dance in the kitchen together while the rice boils over on the stove. You're interested in knowing if, this far in, we're all about routine or if we still have a glimmer of romance. By the way, the answer to all those questions would be *yes* which is nothing less than a miracle considering the roller coaster we've ridden together. But, as we'll stumble onto later, how we feel about Jesus has a dramatic effect on how we feel about other people. Push hold on that for now.

We don't give a second thought to characterizing love primarily by feelings in our human relationships but, somehow, when it comes to Jesus, the definition shifts. The difference is understandable, of course. He is not visible. It's easy to subconsciously conclude that, since Jesus is unseeable, love for Jesus is probably unfeelable. With this view, love for Jesus is most about doing and least about feeling. Not only is this view misleading, it's woefully dissatisfying. In fact, Christ's point with Simon Peter in their dialogue in John 21 was that *the doing* He was assigning him ("feed My sheep") could only be sustained and satisfied for the long haul through *the loving*.

We're not talking about hyper-emotion and learning to levitate ourselves into spiritual hysteria with Jesus. That would no more be the goal in our relationship with Him than it would be the goal in a marriage. Keith Moore put a ring on my finger thirty-six solid years ago. My affection for him often enough spikes feverishly, especially on sentimental occasions, or when I get home after several days away, or in a happy resolution after a big fat fight. Sometimes it spikes for no reason at all and takes me by surprise. But even in seasons between the fever-pitch, my relationship with Keith is overwhelmingly defined by a feeling. I *feel* a way about him that I do not *feel* about another person on the planet. My love for him, as flawed as I am, is too big to hide in my heart. It surfaces in skin and shows up in actions. Because I love him, I like to do things for him, but, if he asked me if I loved him, his heart would sink if I responded, "I cooked you dinner last night, didn't I?" Try to picture Christ asking Peter if he loved Him and Peter saying, "I swam to You, didn't I?"

The love Jesus longs for is not just devotion. It's also emotion.

It's not just volition. It is also affection.

It is not just discipline. It is also passion.

It's not just routine. It is also romance.

And not just for Christ's sake but also for ours. Love is the catalyst. The holy cause and effect. We'll see that together in the chapters to come but I want to say something to you about you as we narrow this one to a close.

The person you are when you love Jesus with everything in you—with your whole heart, soul, mind, and strength—is the real you. The brilliant you. The *bring-it* you. The breathtaking you. The *born-for-this* you. The person you were born to be crawls out of the shell of a heart cracked wide-open to the audacious love of Christ. When your heart, your soul, your mind, and might are engaged in a wholly invasive holy affection, march yourself into the nearest bathroom and look in the mirror over the sink.

That's you.

And what *that* woman in *that* mirror in *that* condition of teeming affection most wants to do is most likely *that* woman's calling or the carrier of *that* direction. Does *that* woman in *that* mirror want to help the homeless, teach kindergartners, visit shut-ins, teach Bible classes, reach the unreached, write a book, work on an album, foster children, go to seminary, work with preteen girls, tutor underprivileged kids, work in law enforcement, fight human trafficking, finish creating that cookbook, pursue an acting career, become a college professor, manage money for nonprofits, run a corporation, do medical missions, volunteer at a women's shelter, or be a network news anchor?

When the blood in your veins runs hot with holy affection for the living Christ, what do you want to do most? Paul put it this way: *Christ's love compels us.*[3] When Christ's love invades every cell in your body, what are you compelled to do? The follow-up question is critical. The answer to it is where the rubber meets the road, where dreams become realities and destinies that defy gravity finally get fulfilled. This is it: What would it take to do it? You answer those two questions: *What are you most compelled by the love of Christ to do?* and *What would it take to do it?*—then identify one first step toward that direction, and, child, you will find the next place to plant your foot on your divinely planned path.

Don't tell me you're too young. Don't tell me you're too old. Don't tell me you're too scared. Don't tell me you're too busy. Get to it. Nobody but you can do it.

---

3. 2 Cor. 5:14 NIV

Getting to Something Definitive

What you and I need is a working definition of the word this book is all about so that, every time we use it, we have a clear picture of what it looks like lived out. If we're going to *audaciously love*, we better find out how to recognize ourselves when we're doing it. Nobody can help us with a definition like *Merriam-Webster*. You have to give credit where credit is due. After all, Noah Webster went to all the trouble to learn twenty-six languages so that he could get a proper enough grasp on the etymology of words to have the guts to produce his first dictionary in 1828.[1] That takes some commitment. You might say he possessed a bonus supply of the very thing we're looking to define. Below is the definition of our key word from the latest edition of Mr. Webster's publishing descendants. Add an *ly* to the end of it and—*voilá*—it will turn into our adverb.

Here you go:

---

1. About Noah Webster, accessed online at http://www.merriam-webster.com/info/noah.htm.

au•da•cious \ȯ-'dā-shəs\ *adjective*
[Middle French *audacieux*, from *audace* boldness, from Latin
audacia, from *audac-*, *audax* bold, from *audēre* to dare, from
avidus eager . . .]
1 a: intrepidly daring: ADVENTUROUS (an *audacious* mountain
climber)
b: recklessly bold: RASH (an *audacious* maneuver)
2: contemptuous of law, religion, or decorum: INSOLENT
3: marked by originality and verve (*audacious* experiments)—
au•da•cious•ly *adverb*—**au•da•cious•ness** *noun*[2]

Audacious is a fabulous word, don't you think? It's a word with an aerobic
heart rate if you'll ever find one. A word with a closet full of running shoes
and pointe shoes, of rock-climbing gear and hiking boots. It's the kind of
word that can get a person up and moving in the morning without hitting
the snooze alarm fourteen times. It's the extra shot of espresso in your cap-
puccino and it doesn't come in decaf. It's the kind of word that can go with
anyone to work anywhere because it's about perspective, not performance.
But make no mistake. It's a perspective that profoundly affects performance.
Anything that makes a home in our brains finds a way to our bones.

To keep our working definition of our term consistent with the character and teachings of the one we aim to love audaciously, we'll scratch
through the second definition and two additional words and still have
everything we need to embrace:

au•da•cious \ȯ-'dā-shəs\ *adjective*
[Middle French *audacieux*, from *audace* boldness, from Latin
audacia, from *audac-*, *audax* bold, from *audēre* to dare, from
avidus eager . . .]

2. Frederick C. Mish, ed., *Merriam-Webster's Collegiate Dictionary* (Springfield, MA: Merriam-
Webster, Inc. (2003), 80.

1 a: intrepidly daring: ADVENTUROUS (an *audacious* mountain climber)
b: ~~recklessly~~ bold: ~~rash~~ (an *audacious* maneuver)
2: ~~contemptuous of law, religion, or decorum: INSOLENT~~
3: marked by originality and verve (*audacious* experiments)—
au•da•cious•ly *adverb*—**au•da•cious•ness** *noun*[3]

We could have pushed and prodded some of those scratched-out words into appropriate enough applications but constantly qualifying them would reduce the clarity we need in order to move forward with traction. We want this thing to be clear. We also want it to be consistent with Scripture or we'll end up with a goal that shoots off like a bottle rocket into nothing but bushes—and throws us into a whole different trajectory than God's very thought-out goal for us. Talk about counterproductive. We want a goal God can support because what He supports, He brings to pass. In this context, He brings it to pass *through us*.

He'll supply the supernatural strength, the open doors, the opportunities, the abounding grace, His own indwelling Spirit, the incentives, the instructions, the insight and discernment, the divine energy, the people, the partners, the favor and every single miracle necessary to accomplish it. He'll kick down obstacles with His own foot, back off enemies with His own elbows, and blow the wind of the Spirit on us with His own breath. When we get behind the same goal God has for us, we're going to get all the provision we need because the credit's preapproved. That's no small thing. That's what you call a guarantee.

Each part of the remaining definition of *Webster's audacious* will pop up before we put down this book but it all launches with the first synonym. Glance back at the very beginning of the definition and you'll find

---

3. Ibid.

the terms our word *audacious* comes from. See the Middle French word *audace*? It translates into English as boldness. We'd find almost no end to all the examples of God-blessed *boldness* in the Bible and far more than my commitment to a short book makes room to mention. But since we're women and some of us might be tempted to think that God-authorized boldness is more fitting for men, I'll throw out a handful of names.

Take Miriam, for example. She was the young teenage daughter of slave-class parents during the reign of a Pharaoh who'd decided to curb the burgeoning population of Jews by slaughtering all their baby boys. If you've heard the story many times, slow down with it this time and try to wrap your mind around it. Can you fathom the horror and grief? When her parents couldn't hide her baby brother any longer, they put him in a basket waterproofed with pitch and stuck it in the reeds by a riverbank. Miriam stood at a distance and watched with bated breath to see if he'd somehow be saved, all the while risking that he may be silenced with a sword right before her eyes. The daughter of the murderous Pharaoh came down to the river to bathe and discovered the wailing infant. That young slave-class girl had the chutzpah to break every rule of social decorum, walk right up to Pharaoh's daughter, and offer to fetch a Hebrew woman to nurse the child until he was weaned. And the princess complied. That's boldness.

Then there's Deborah, "a mother in Israel"[4] and a prophetess who served as a judge for the people of God during a time of Canaanite oppression. She summoned a man named Barak to take military leadership over the army of Israel and launch an aggressive campaign against the Canaanite forces led by a commander named Sisera. Barak responded that he'd do it if she'd go to war next to him but, otherwise, she could find herself somebody else. She stepped up and went to war beside him.

---

4. Judg. 5:7

When the enemy forces approached their army with 900 iron chariots and an intimidating slew of warriors, she said to Barak,

"Move on, for this is the day the LORD has handed Sisera over to you. Hasn't the LORD gone before you?" So Barak came down from Mount Tabor with 10,000 men following him. The LORD threw Sisera, all his charioteers, and all his army into confusion with the sword before Barak. Sisera left his chariot and fled on foot. (Judg. 4:14–15)

There's also Abigail whose rapid reaction, stunning composure, and ingenious counsel kept her whole household from getting killed.[5] And it would be a shame not to mention Ruth, a young widow from the land of Moab who refused to let Naomi, her widowed mother-in-law, return to her homeland of Bethlehem without her. If Ruth didn't win the worthy heart of a landowner named Boaz by applying a little boldness, I don't know what you call it. You'll want to read that account for yourself in the third chapter of Ruth. It's better than nighttime television. The point is, we girls can forget using gender as an excuse for our lack of holy audacity.

Now, let's flip to the New Testament and pick out a few times when the synonym *boldness* shows up on the page.

*When they observed the **boldness** of Peter and John and realized that they were uneducated and untrained men, they were amazed and recognized that they had been with Jesus.* (Acts 4:13, emphasis mine)

---

5. 1 Sam. 25

Did you see that? To live the life we long for, we want people around us to recognize with their chins dropped that we have something beyond what our education and training can explain. That goes for you even if you earned a doctorate. Our lives were meant to exceed what a natural course of events could explain. We want people to see that, what we have, we could only get from being with Jesus. God used one thing in that Acts 4 scene to draw the attention of the observers to Peter and John: *boldness*. But that wasn't the only time boldness was at play, here's another one:

> *When they had prayed, the place where they were assembled was shaken, and they were all filled with the Holy Spirit and began to speak God's message with **boldness**.* (Acts 4:31, emphasis mine)

Please glare at the barefaced fact that the filling of the Holy Spirit is tied directly and without a single knot or fray to the boldness all those people possessed to speak God's message. They, too, were surrounded by a culture hostile to the gospel but they had discovered a driving force more powerful than their fear. We're going to discover it, too. In case you're getting a little worried that we could all turn out loud-mouthed, rude and crude, this is a good time for me to state emphatically that boldness as a God-stamped quality in the life of a believer never cancels out humility or love *or* a bearable volume. Remember, our primary aim is to tie every bit of this concept into our affections toward Jesus Christ and, through the sieve of His person, to all others in our relational sphere. In Christ's economy, bold never means cold. Let's keep going.

> *Then [Paul] stayed two whole years in his own rented house. And he welcomed all who visited him, proclaiming the kingdom of God*

and teaching the things concerning the Lord Jesus Christ with full **boldness** *and without hindrance.* (Acts 28:30–31, emphasis mine)

How about that? *Full* boldness that was, at the very same time, welcoming. That's how we're also meant to live, speak, and serve people. Boldness says that we don't see every little obstacle as some big hindrance. We're not too fragile to adapt and too finicky to accept. Boldness says that each circumstance is up for rent as opportunity. What we're willing to do with the room we've been given is up to us. Boldness makes the best of it.

And another:

Therefore, having such a hope, we use great **boldness**. (2 Cor. 3:12, emphasis mine)

Did you catch the connection between hope and boldness in that one? If you and I are going to live and love audaciously, we're going to have to quit answering the door when hopelessness bangs its ugly fist at it. It has no place in our lives. Hopelessness is a liar. A convincing one. We offer it no welcome, no couch to rest upon, no meal to feast upon. We do not cater to it in any way. All the enemy of our souls would have to do is to kick the legs of audacity out from under us and fuel our souls with hopelessness. If we're followers of Christ, we're not even hopeless when we stare imminent death right in the scary face. Case in point from Paul's ink pen under the threat of death in prison:

My eager expectation and hope is that I will not be ashamed about anything, but that now as always, with all **boldness**, *Christ will be* *highly honored in my body, whether by life or by death.* (Phil. 1:20, emphasis mine)

Not only is God calling us to live boldly, He wants us to die boldly. This holy audacity that we're seeking in these pages can carry us all the way to our dying breath. Listen, it takes some audacity to die well. If we're going to die anyway—and we are if Jesus tarries—we might as well do it audaciously. If we do, that very same verse states that Christ will be *highly honored.* That's a pretty powerful incentive.

Can you handle one more? Then let's make it this one:

*Therefore let us approach the throne of grace with **boldness**, so that we may receive mercy and find grace to help us at the proper time.* (Heb. 4:16, emphasis mine)

If you're new to a life with Jesus, the "throne of grace" is where God is seated as sovereign king and possessor of things. The picture this verse paints is of a king who makes Himself astonishingly accessible. Night and day. He's never off. Never distracted. Never texting while we're talking. Here is the verse in its context and with its cause.

*Therefore, since we have a great high priest who has passed through the heavens—Jesus the Son of God—let us hold fast to the confession. For we do not have a high priest who is unable to sympathize with our weaknesses, but One who has been tested in every way as we are, yet without sin. Therefore let us approach the throne of grace with **boldness**, so that we may receive mercy and find grace to help us at the proper time.* (Heb. 4:14–16, emphasis mine)

Jesus is able to sympathize with our weaknesses. Every last one of them. He, fully God, subjected Himself to flesh and blood—to hunger, to thirst, to weariness, to rejection, to betrayal, to grief, to mockery, to unimaginable suffering, and ultimately to death—to be tested in every way we are. Stack those among the reasons why it's hard to find a lot not to like about Him.

Because the eternal purpose of God was fully accomplished in Jesus,[6] we are authorized, urged, exhorted, and expected to approach His throne with absolute boldness.

Confidently. *Audaciously.* Like we believe what He says. Like we receive what He's done. Like we accept who we are. Like we know what it took. The exorbitant price He paid for our access is worthy of nothing less.

If we've got it in our heads that God gets a kick out of us cowering and groveling at His feet, no wonder we recoil from Him. We've created a god in the human image of a savage dictator driven by hate who licks his lips at the sight of our wounds and is sickly empowered by the pleas of the powerless. We'll never audaciously love a god like that. And God help us, we shouldn't. *That god* is not ours. The God of the Bible has no lust for power because He has no lack of power. He is not built up by us being torn down. God does not get the most pleasure when we are the most pathetic.

We're starting to sketch a picture of what audacity would look like wearing our clothes. It's not pale. It's not pasty. It doesn't look best in pastels. It's bold.

---

6. Eph. 3:11–12

The First Audacious Move

Maybe any of many roads would take us to our goal of audaciously following Christ. We're going for a certain methodology that I've seen, studied, and experienced but, no doubt, others could land us in a spot with a similar outcome. The launch point, however, is nonnegotiable. An audacious love that would light our hearts up like a torch catches fire from one source alone. To audaciously love, we must—to the last atom in our DNA—believe that we are audaciously *loved*. The fire spreads no other way.

I'm not asking you today if you believe Jesus loves you. Some of us were singing "Jesus Loves Me" before we had a clue who we were talking about. I'm not knocking that. I wouldn't trade those lyrics or hearing my toddlers crooning every line from the top of their lungs in the backseat of our old station wagon. But you and I are trying to press past our automatic answers in this book. I'm asking you if you believe our adverb could sit next to His affection for you. Do you believe with unrelenting conviction and confidence that Jesus *audaciously* loves you? Are you convinced that a fiery passion rages within Him toward you?

It's so much easier to believe He loves somebody else like that but, right now, this is about Jesus and you and nobody else. Everything starts here. If it doesn't and you assimilate into your belief system that you are more passionate about Jesus than He is about you, performance will overtake passion and frustration will supplant satisfaction. You'll get your feelings hurt by Him constantly and, after you've put yourself out there long enough, you will feel burned and charred by overexposure and withdraw.

We cannot out-love Jesus because love is not just something He does. It's something He *is*.[1] He is incapable of loving less because He is incapable of being less. Our devotion and emotion at the spire of their Everest cannot rake the tip of His. Jesus is always the initiator in every aspect of our relationship with Him. Every time you are driven to pursue Him, it's because He is pursuing you. Every time you have something to say to Him, it's because He's saying something to you. Every time you choose Him, He has already chosen you. Any time you get up before dawn and head into your den to pray, He is already there waiting for you. You never have a single thought about Him that catches His mind wandering away from you. You cannot beat Jesus to the punch. You cannot beat Jesus to the passion. Hear the words from Eugene Peterson's translation of 1 John 4:19.

> *We, though, are going to love—love and be loved. First we were loved, now we love. He loved us first.* (The Message)

Jesus does not feel the same way about you that you do. You may like yourself one minute and hate yourself the next but that's because

---

1. 1 John 4:8

you're not Jesus. Neither am I. He's not moody. He's not subject to hormones. He also hasn't loved us so long that He's settled into a nice, steady, energy-saving medium. Let's quit painting Jesus with the expression of a male version of the Mona Lisa. His love is eternal and infinite, fiery and feverish. Audacious.

Remember that definition in our last chapter? Let's glance at it again—but, this time, in simpler form, leaving out the terms we scratched from it:

Audacious:
intrepidly daring, adventurous,
bold,
marked by originality and verve.

His love for you is like that. It always has been. Always will be. In our second chapter, we talked about the small word *all* and practiced a little audacity by sticking it right in front of the word *women* in the vision statement. We could have done the same with the word *men. All* is a three-letter word with the power to knock down walls between genders, push through doors in closed countries, bypass caste systems and social structures, displace stereotypes and prejudices, and insult arrogance and exclusivity. According to the Scriptures, Christ gave His life as a ransom for *all* and the gospel invitation is extended to *all*.

For the grace of God has appeared with salvation for all people.
(Titus 2:11)

But the wonder of salvation occurs with *each* who receive it. Read this portion of Romans 1:16 carefully then jump back on that compound word in the middle line.

For I am not ashamed of the gospel, because it is God's power for salvation to everyone who believes.

Everyone = every *one*. Salvation takes the gospel personally. If you're really familiar with the concept, don't go into automatic here. This train of thought has a tie to our concept that is absolutely key. Give me a couple of pages to show you how. Salvation declares that I do not only believe that Jesus came for all. I believe He also came for me. I do not only believe that Jesus gave His life for all. I believe He gave His life for me. And I receive it and all its implications. This personalization to the fullest extent of Christ's coming unearths the vivid reality that we are not just loved by Him. We are audaciously loved by Him.

Boldly. Daringly. Adventurously.

Think this through and see if those adverbs find any fitting place to land.

The Son of God existed in timelessness with the Father and the Holy Spirit. Out of their glorious, unspeakable oneness and fellowship, they spun a plan into motion to create mortal beings in their image. This plan would involve a universe comprised of millions of galaxies and necessitate the perfect placement and tilt of a single planet in a solar system where it could support and sustain life.

For this is what the LORD says—
God is the Creator of the heavens.
He formed the earth and made it.
He established it;
He did not create it to be empty,
but formed it to be inhabited. (Isa. 45:18)

The Eternal One knew the end from the beginning and foresaw what would be as clear as if it had already been. The fall of man would happen early on and, if the Godhead had no intention for redemption, the Word that would speak the planets into orbit might as well save His breath. Would the Father be willing to let the Son out of His arms and release Him to an orb heaving and quaking with sin? Would they be willing to do what salvation would take? Would they be willing to pay what redemption would cost?

And they were.

Before God said, "Let there be light," the plan was already drawn: "Let there be the cross." And, in the words of Revelation 13:8, the Son became *the Lamb slain from the foundation of the world.*[2] The moment God formed man from the dust of the ground and breathed into his nostrils the breath of life, the die was cast, the cross previewed, and the body-to-come of the eternal Son was, as they say, as good as dead.

The clock that had no place in timelessness took its first tick and appointed something strange and titillating: *a beginning.* Call that originality. And *in the beginning God created the heavens and the earth.* Generations came and generations went, patriarchs raised and a reluctant deliverer sent. Through wonders, theophanies, and glimpses of glory, God

---

2. KJV

revealed Himself to mortal man and pledged to dwell among His people. The Law was given and the breath of God began to come upon men to put pen to story. As the story goes, the people rebelled in the wilderness, their hearts like golden calves. Consequences came but God never left. A few days turned to forty years and the carcasses of the faithless were bleached white by the desert sun. Under the valiant command of Joshua, their sons and daughters crossed the River Jordan, and entered the land of promise, a land of milk and honey. A land where giants fell and former losers won.

For a while, that is. Eventually they lost interest in the victory-giver and chose the thrill of the mudslide from extraordinariness to ordinariness and on down to oppression. Judges sprang up to lead the people but primarily, it seemed, into sin. Ultimately "everyone did what was right in his own eyes."[3] Judges were followed by kings, and among the kings, one after God's own heart. David—the psalmist, shepherd, soldier—to whom this promise of God was given through the prophet Nathan:

Your house and kingdom will endure before Me forever,
and your throne will be established forever. (2 Sam. 7:16)

David died, as did his sons, and then the sons of his sons. A kingdom divided turned from God and embraced the idols of other nations. The people of God—both north and south—were carried into captivity just as his prophets foretold. Through a God-ordained decree, a remnant returned to Jerusalem and began to rebuild and life of a lesser glory resumed within her walls. Then the time the prophet Amos foretold came to pass.

---

3. Judg. 21:25 (ESV)

Hear this! The days are coming—
this is the declaration of the Lord GOD—
when I will send a famine through the land:
not a famine of bread or a thirst for water,
but of hearing the words of the LORD.[4]

And the scroll of the Old Testament rolled out to its full measure and stopped at the final margin. The ink dried and the mouth of God fell silent for four centuries. But only to the ears of the earthbound. Imagine the divine dialogue. There is no record of it. All is conjecture. But press into the possibilities with me. Try to grasp the patience of the Godhead to meticulously unfold the plan of redemption one generation at a time and one revelation at a time. A Father, so taken with His Son and anxious to show Him off, had shown generations of men one snapshot after another as if to say, "He looks a little like this." A little like Isaac. A little like Joseph. A little like Moses. A little like Joshua. A little like David. To some like Ezekiel and Daniel, He gave glimpses of His Son through visions that were so awe-striking that the bodies of both men buckled at the sight.

But a new era was now on the horizon. Through all the years of divine silence on earth, the fellowship of the Father, Son, and Holy Spirit never ceased in heaven. Together they would have been watching the terrestrial clock with rapt attention.

The days turned into weeks. The weeks turned into months. The months turned into years. The years turned into decades. The decades turned into one century.

Then two.

---

4. Amos 8:11

Then three.

Three ran like the wind toward four.

Did the seconds of the last year of that final silent century pound like a hammer with hurried fury in the heavens? This moment had been anticipated since God covered Adam and Eve in animal skins and cast them from the Garden. This moment was in the mind of God when He called a man named Abram then substituted a ram on the altar for the life of his son, Isaac. This moment was foretold when God promised King David an everlasting kingdom. The *set time* for the moment had finally *fully come*. So,

> *. . . when the set time had fully come, God sent his Son, born of a woman.*[5]

Imagine it: Christ, there in the heavens in the company of His Father, surrounded by angels of unfathomable grandeur and the time comes for Him to go. The apex of the plan of redemption set in motion before the foundation of the world was next on the docket. What would it have been like to be God and agree to become man? To be the infinite Creator[6] and confine yourself to skin? *For in him the whole fullness of deity dwells bodily.*[7] You would not be agreeing to take on the flesh of a grown man like the first one you'd formed with your own hands. You'd be the Son of God and fully God consenting to become a microscopic embryo in a young woman's womb.

The whole thing is incomprehensible. According to Scripture, even the angels could not wrap their minds around the plan for the salvation

---

5. Gal. 4:4 NIV
6. Col. 1:15–17
7. Col. 2:9 ESV

of man.[8] So, when the time had fully come for Christ to go, were there good-byes? Last looks back? Did the hosts of heaven watch as the Holy Spirit overshadowed a young teenage girl? Then, at that very moment, did Christ suddenly disappear from their sight?

Unfathomably, the words of David in Psalm 139 then broke the barriers of natural law and ricocheted from the mortal body of the holy, eternal Son of God:

For it was You who created my inward parts;
You knit me together in my mother's womb.
I will praise You
because I have been remarkably and wonderfully made.
Your works are wonderful,
and I know this very well.
My bones were not hidden from You
when I was made in secret,
when I was formed in the depths of the earth.
Your eyes saw me when I was formless;
all my days were written in Your book and planned
before a single one of them began.[9]

The Son of God, conceived by the Holy Spirit, born of a virgin: He rolled over for the first time perhaps somewhere around four months old. He crawled and toddled. He skinned His knees. The one called *the Word* learned to talk. He lost His baby teeth and, for a while, may have even lisped. He laughed and cried. Got tickled and sobbed. He, who'd never slumbered, slept and He, who'd never hungered, ate. The rest of the story

---

8. 1 Pet. 1:12
9. Ps. 139:13–16

is written in permanent marker on the pages of the New Testament. Jesus grew into manhood and walked on callous feet of flesh to the banks of the Jordan River. There in the waters He'd once parted for the children of Israel, John the Baptizer dunked His head.

After Jesus was baptized, He went up immediately from the water. The heavens suddenly opened for Him, and He saw the Spirit of God descending like a dove and coming down on Him. And there came a voice from heaven:

This is My beloved Son.
I take delight in Him! (Matt. 3:16–17)

Come on, now. Does a story get any better than that? Well, yes. As a matter of fact, it does. He went to a wedding and turned water into wine. He cleansed lepers, healed the sick, played with the children, gave sight to the blind, unstopped the ears of the deaf, stood up the bent-over, and loosed tongues of the mute. He stood at the edge of the Sea of Galilee and looked amid the waves to a boatful of disciples frantically fighting the wind in the spooky dark. He could have parted the waters like He'd done before and made it to them on dry land, but He saved Himself the trouble this time. He just stepped right on top of the waves and walked.

He confounded the wise, called the simple, dined with sinners, dipped bread with a betrayer, and took up for the looked-down upon. He cursed a fig tree, rode a donkey, cast demons out right and left and into pigs and off a cliff. He fed thousands from a few fish and loaves and preached the Scriptures to multitudes and droves.

And He raised the dead.

Then, He did what He'd come most to do. Sweating blood, He submitted Himself to the will of His Father to give over His life and hang on a cross, letting the full weight of humanity's sin rest bloody and mean on His body. He cried out "It is finished!" then He bowed His head and gave up His Spirit.

Stone cold dead.

Three days later, He sat straight up and walked out of that tomb. He appeared to His disciples and some five hundred others and, after a period of forty days, entrusted the gospel to His followers, promised to send the Holy Spirit for comfort and power, and ascended right before their eyes straight up into the heavens. Don't you know they were glad to get Him home?

Dear God.

If that's not adventure, I don't know it. If that's not bold, I can't picture it. If that's not daring, we can't decipher it. If that's not originality and verve, we'll never discover it.

That is audacious. Here's the part that connects the point straight to you. John 3:16–17 tells us exactly why the Father sent His only beloved Son:

> *For God so loved the world that He gave His only begotten Son, that whoever believes in Him should not perish but have everlasting life. For God did not send His Son into the world to condemn the world, but that the world through Him might be saved.* (NKJV)

The world in those two verses does not refer to soil and springs and sand and seas. It refers to people. Rewind with me to the beginning of this chapter and remember the proposal that salvation takes the gospel personally. That means, if you have the guts to do it, you get to stand before this glorious plan, behold, and say, "For God so loved *me* that He gave His only begotten Son."

He knew your name before creation. He knew all your life would entail. He knew both strands of your DNA by heart. He appointed the color of your eyes and the prints of your fingers. He chose the generation in which you'd live and planted you in an exact spot on the planet to initiate divine purpose.[10] He enacted a plan of epic proportions that would include you. His Son took on flesh for all humankind, yes. But that includes you. He gave His life for you. He rose from the dead for you. He sits at the right hand of God to intercede for you. He sent His promised Holy Spirit to seal, sanctify, thrill, and fill you.

Every single day Jesus pursues you. Every single day Jesus fights valiantly for you. Every single day He gazes on your face and brings you one step closer to seeing His.

Do you have the audacity to take what He's done personally? Do you have the audacity to believe to your bones that He has adventurously, daringly, and boldly pursued you with a passion as fiery red as blood? That His temperature toward you has not decreased a solitary degree? That *Jesus Christ is the same yesterday, today, and forever* (Heb. 13:8)?

To get where you and I are headed, we're going to have to become shameless about the way Jesus feels toward us. I do mean *shameless*. You'll never find a more perfect synonym for audacious. Shame and audacity cannot coexist. They cannot consume the same space. God is not mistaking our shame for humility. People who cover over the blood of Christ with a cloak of shame do no honor to the name of Jesus. He doesn't pat us on the head and say, "You poor sweet things." If we're going to insist on keeping all our shame after all He's done, we can save ourselves the

10. Acts 17:26–27

trouble of pursuing audacious love because we'll have no place to put it. We'll never be freed up to love Jesus audaciously if we're living our lives as one big apology.

But, if we're willing to give up our addiction to shame,

to believe what He's done,

to receive His full redemption

and the forgiveness of all our sins,

and consider ourselves outrageously loved

and valiantly pursued,

we, my friend, are about to run free in the wide-open liberty of audacity.

Waking the Dead

The day I turned thirty, I got to attend my own funeral. A friend showed up at my house late that morning insisting that I get in the car with her and accompany her to an undisclosed location. Relieved that I'd not been caught in my pajamas without my mascara and deodorant on or with my massive untamed hair resembling something akin to a mad squirrel's nest, I went along rather happily. After all, I was expecting a surprise party.

When one gets picked up on one's thirtieth birthday and one's husband appears suspiciously unsurprised, that is what one expects. One does not expect a funeral. Such a thought would not enter one's mind. However, in this case, it happened to enter the conniving minds of a room full of lively women around my same age who attended the Sunday school class I taught each week.

After about a twenty-minute drive with significantly less chatter than I'm accustomed to, my friend wound through a lovely neighborhood then pulled into a driveway and turned off the ignition. I grinned. It was obviously party time and, based on the number of cars parked at the curb, it would be no small party. *How sweet*, I thought to myself. I

knew the drill. We'd walk through the door and they'd yell, "*Surprise!*"
And then I would act, well, *surprised.*

We walked through the door to a room full of women, but no one
yelled, "*Surprise!*" In fact, no one even looked at me. Not one person
acknowledged that I was in the room, including, all the sudden, the friend
who'd picked me up at my own house and driven me halfway across town.
Once she shoved me down in a particular chair, she developed amnesia.
Organ music was playing—the likes of which you're mostly forced to
hear at a funeral home. All the women were dressed in black, seated
in carefully ordered rows of chairs—coiffed and cosmeticized like old-
school church ladies who lacked sufficient sight to hit their lips with their
lip-liners. Never in your life have you ever seen more lipstick on pairs of
front teeth. Many of the congregants had on hats and gloves and were
clutching hankies. Others were passing around tissues and sympatheti-
cally patting each other's hands.

Finally the music faded and a woman walked ceremoniously to the
front, set a Bible on the podium, and began to officiate the service with a
face so straight, she could have won a fortune playing poker. The moment
she took the floor, I knew good and well that she'd instigated the whole
thing. She was just the one clever and creative and authoritative enough
to pull it off. She commenced to deliver a eulogy in which she'd master-
fully woven every embarrassing thing I'd ever said or done in front of
that class. Furthermore, she did so mimicking my quirky mannerisms of
which there are no few. She'd clearly practiced. The woman was a dead
ringer of the dearly departed even to the dearly departed.

Several women were called forth from the audience to also say a few
words in memoriam. The histrionics knew no bounds. Every story was a
kernel of truth stirred into a heaping helping of artistic license. The skit
could have won an Emmy. The whole thing was *Saturday Night Live*

meets Sunday school. At dramatic highpoints, the crowd would erupt into wailing and nose-blowing of such impressive volume that, had it been winter, the honking could well have called in a flock of Canadian geese.

It was perfect. You can't wrap my favorite kind of gifts in pretty boxes and put bows on them. My favorite gifts are memories. And, boy, did I ever get a room full of gifts for my thirtieth birthday. Those women went so far as to sign a funeral guestbook as my greeting card. You can't say that's not love.

I've thought about that day a thousand times. What that class of loons concocted was so well thought-out and hilarious that I'll never forget it. It was also surreal. Imagine being a spectator at a mock-up of your own memorial service and no one acknowledging that you are there. It's like spending a minute or two in the pointy-toed shoes of Ebenezer Scrooge.

But say, for a moment, we really could listen in on our own memorial service. Don't get all morose on me. Just think fictionally with me for a few minutes and picture, perhaps, a day many, many years from now at the end of a good, long life. Set aside any sense of tragedy surrounding your earthly exit so you're free to think this through without feeling depressed. Imagine that you're in your nineties, ready to walk out of your aching feet and looking forward to some really fabulous new hair . . . and that you simply get to fall asleep and wake up to the face of Jesus.

The next thing you know, you're in a theater seat with a bucket of buttered popcorn in your lap and your memorial service starts rolling right there on the silver screen. Your favorite singer finishes up your favorite song and everybody in the on-screen audience forgets decorum and breaks out in applause. They can't help themselves. It was all they could do not to somersault down the aisles. A man with a particularly commanding presence walks up to the podium, sets a Bible on it with a dramatic thud, then pans the audience intently from the left of the room to the right.

He pulls out the program with the order of service your family meticulously prepared and printed from a template they found on the web. It's the same program the usher handed to each of the attendees as they signed the guestbook and walked through the door. Since we get to script this scene any way we want, let's make the program full-color. Personally, I've never seen a full-color order of service but this is a really great funeral. Remember, your favorite vocal artist just sang the hair off of everybody's arms. This is a 5-star funeral you're hosting here.

The very distinguished guy at the podium pulls out the full-color program and waves it so dramatically in front of the audience that bangs blow on the front row. It should go without saying that your picture is on the front of the program. Not one of you at twenty-one, either, the practice of which is always a mystery to me at a funeral of someone who'd managed to survive Planet Earth's killer instincts and make it to a well-advanced age. I read somewhere that your basic used kitchen sponge has about twelve million bacteria in it. That we live past scrubbing our first plate is a wonder never ceasing. Reaching old age is worth some hearty acknowledgment and robust celebration. God help us, the picture on the program at our funerals doesn't have to look like a glamor shot. This place causes a person some wear and tear, some banging up and bruising. A few of them might as well show.

That said, the picture on the front of the program is of you at full age—your life completely lived. You'll have a new body by then so you won't care. Consider the juxtaposition as the ultimate *before and after*. The man at the podium points to that picture and says with perfect diction and powerful conviction, "You see that woman right there?"

Everybody nods.

"She was intrepidly daring," he states emphatically. He might have even rolled his r's.

A number of *Amens* pipe up around the room. All sorts of people look at one another and say things like, "She sure as heck was" and "That's a fact."

Then the officiant still up front says, "That woman was adventurous."

Someone shouts out, "That was her alright!" Loud *uh-huhs* lilt around the room.

After observing a pregnant pause for just the right effect, he adds, "Bold!"

By this point everybody's working up into a lather.

Now he holds your picture out in front of the audience with both hands, paper crisp and taut, and, in the tone used at a national convention to announce a political party candidate for the president of the United States, the officiant at your service booms, "That woman had *verve!*" You're sure he rolled his r's this time.

The crowd goes wild. Fist pumping. Cheering. Applauding. Two-finger whistling. A cowbell from the back. One woman pulls a tambourine out of her patent leather purse and takes to the aisle. Another one rushes the platform and pulls the Rose of Sharon flag out of its stand and runs with it like the wind. Sprays fall off their stands.

Maybe the funeral crowd wouldn't be quite that raucous but they should be. If those words really did describe you, somebody ought to be clapping about it. Somebody ought to cough up an *Amen*. Some young woman ought to lean over and whisper to the person sitting next to her, "She loved and lived as audaciously as anybody I've ever seen. I want to be like her."

When your life is said and done, don't you wish someone would say that you were adventurous and daring? That you really lived this thing? That you weren't too scared of your own shadow to chase the shadow of Christ even if it took you to Madagascar? Or, just across the tracks to the rough side of town? In chapter 4, we slashed through synonyms like insolent, contemptuous, and rash in *Webster's* definition of *audacious* so you know we aren't talking about being adventurously and daringly dumb. We're talking about bodacious bravery and being up for a challenge and not excusing and comforting and protecting ourselves right out of our reasons for being here.

I hope to prove to you in the rest of this chapter and in pages to come that, according to Scripture, *loving* audaciously is the shoo-in for *living* audaciously. If you love Jesus audaciously, you won't have to worry about whether or not you live audaciously. The one calls the other forth like an irresistible herald. Your feet will follow your fiery heart. You will reach the end of your mortal life having lived out a real, live, bona fide adventure even if you don't realize just how much until Jesus rolls tape from the zoom lens of heaven. Courage comes from the heart. The English word itself comes from the Latin word *cor* that translates *heart*. A heart that audaciously loves beats in the chest of a girl who audaciously lives.

What all of us could use right now is a big, fat dose of bravery. Being a woman in a culture that defines valuable as sensual is scary. Refusing to compete in the online game of pretense is scary. Resisting the maelstrom of self-marketing in social media is scary. Somebody might forget we're here. Taking the risk of failing or looking foolish as you figure out *who* God has placed you on this planet to be and *what* He's placed you on this planet to do is scary. An inevitable part of discovering what we're good at is discovering what we're not. Anyone you see out there putting their gifts and experiences to full use with profound effectiveness has had a lion's share of misses. They fell forward as often as they leapt forward.

Even when we land with both feet securely on the sidewalk-square of our calling, we will still stumble around with it more often than we hoped. A work of God cannot be mastered by man, no matter how gifted we are. One day we'll think we've got the thing down. The next day we'll wonder what on the ever-loving earth we were smoking. The paradox is that it takes God to actually serve God. In the terminology of Zechariah 4:6, it's *"Not by strength or by might, but by My Spirit," says the* LORD *of Hosts.* We have to trust Someone we cannot see, be empowered by a Holy Spirit we often cannot feel, and go with Someone somewhere we have never been. It's much easier to have the depth of a pair of pink floaties than to take the real plunge.

But love braves it.

And not because love is blind. Sometimes love sees far too well. You'll see with absolute clarity that you are way over your head but you do it anyway, holding your breath, because you know it is the will of God. Audaciously loving Jesus doesn't mean that you don't see the water moccasin on the path in front of you. It means you walk the path anyway—with your heart pounding—even if you do it on your tippy toes. You have to know in advance that danger is inherent in every authentic adventure. You put your snake boots on, zip them up, take a deep breath, and go. Audaciously loving Jesus doesn't mean you have no idea your rock climb is high and steep. It means that you wipe the blood from your nose and keep crawling straight up a slick wall of marble.

If you're scared to death of public speaking and God calls you to be a communicator or throws you up there to tell your story, He doesn't blackout the audience so you won't be afraid. At least He's never done that for me. He calls you to do it anyway with every eye on you while you stand there in front of them breaking a sweat. And then you do it again and again and again until you start pushing through your fear. My friend, Sherry, is a lifelong spotlight-dodger who is shy by nature, but she's having the bug-eyed realization in her early thirties that God is calling her to teach Scripture. In front of people. The other day she told me she has to wear a long skirt so people can't see her knees knocking together. That's the kind of thing you do if you're caught up in a whirlwind of audacious love for Jesus. Because love makes you brave. And Jesus makes it worth it.

Take James 1:12, for instance. Read it carefully, noting the cause and effect.

Happy is the one who endures testing, because when he has proven to be genuine, he will receive the crown of life that God promised to those who love him. (NET)

The end of the verse doesn't say that the person endured because he was tremendously disciplined, particularly strong, or impressively gifted. All three of those are beautiful things but only one cause is given in this verse for enduring the kind of testing that proves an individual genuine enough for the King of all creation to crown: the person loved Him. What won't we do for love?

A heart-pumping love for God: that's what compels us to endure when a time of testing nearly kills us. That's what makes us get back up. That's what keeps us in it when we want to quit. You'll see the same connection in 1 Peter 1:6–8:

⁶You rejoice in this, though now for a short time you have had to struggle in various trials ⁷so that the genuineness of your faith—more valuable than gold, which perishes though refined by fire—may result in praise, glory, and honor at the revelation of Jesus Christ. [8]You love Him, though you have not seen Him. And though not seeing Him now, you believe in Him and rejoice with inexpressible and glorious joy.

Did you notice the loop between testing and proving genuine in both segments? Take a good look at James 1:12 and 1 Peter 1:7 and you can't miss it. We don't have to prove anything to God. He is the *kardiognostes*, the Knower of Hearts.[1] He knows exactly what we're made of and exactly what He invested in us. He knows the immensity of the treasures He tucked way down inside of us in a place that can only be tapped by turmoil. God knows precisely how He gifted us and to what unfathomable degree He empowered us through His own Holy Spirit. He knows to the minutest detail how thoroughly He has equipped us. God cannot be conned. He requires no proof to quell His own curiosity. Confusion is human, not divine. God knows exactly how real or pretentious our faith is.

But we don't. That's the thing. Neither do the people in our homes, our workplaces, our churches, our social environments, or our spheres of influence. Neither do angels or demonic principalities. God tests us to bring out the real us. He tests us to prove our faithfulness to Him in front of a devil who bets we're fakes. God tests us to prove us genuine to *a large cloud of witnesses surrounding us* (Heb. 12:1). For crying out loud, He tests us to prove us genuine to ourselves, the last ones to usually know. God

---

1. Acts 1:24; 2589. καρδιογνώστης kardiognóstēs; gen. kardiognóstou, masc. noun from kardía (2588), heart, and ginóskō (1097), to know. One who knows the heart, searcher of hearts (Acts 1:24; 15:8); Spiros Zodhiates, *The Complete Word Study Dictionary: New Testament* (Chattanooga, TN: AMG Publishers, 2000).

knows what is inside of you. That's the person He's trying to surface. If He's knocking the cover off of you, He's trying to get to the light.

Love not only fuels endurance. It feeds obedience. Look at John 14:15:

"If you love Me, you will keep My commands."

If you have a background of abuse like I do and have fallen victim to a colossal misuse of authority like I have, the thought of obeying anybody's "commands" may make your skin crawl. This is one of the chief reasons why getting to know Jesus intimately through the pages of Scripture is vital. That's where we see His character etched in concrete. God cannot be ungodly. Truth cannot tell a lie. Light cannot make you dark. Holiness cannot poke you full of holes. Everything commanded by God commands blessing. It may come sooner. It may come later. But it will come. His way is the way of wholeness, goodness, rightness, and of glad and gleeful reaping. The wording of Deuteronomy 30:16 takes the warm pulse of the righteous commander:

> *For I am commanding you today to love the LORD your God, to walk in His ways, and to keep His commands, statutes, and ordinances, so that you may live and multiply, and the LORD your God may bless you in the land you are entering to possess.*

We who live on this side of Christ's cross and resurrection dwell under the New Covenant where divine promises find parallels primarily in spiritual terms, which, incidentally, far surpass anything temporal.

Jesus promised that our lives rather than our lands would bear much fruit. He promised that we would have, not just life but life more abundantly. He promised to multiply disciples all over the earth, invading every nation and people group with the gospel before He returns. And He's chosen to do that primarily through His own followers. What He commands, He blesses. It takes some audacity to believe that in a culture chock-full of cynics, but you've got a God-breathed Bible to support it.

Audacious love leads to audacious obedience. And, sooner or later, audacious obedience leads to blessing. Maybe even sooner *and* later. First Timothy 4:8 promises that *godliness is beneficial in every way, since it holds promise for the present life and also for the life to come.*

Listen, you can't live an obedient life and miss an adventure. Following the commands of Christ is not just about behavior. Behavior modification is not an end in itself in the New Testament. Transformation is about knowing the truth and the truth setting you free. If you'll follow Christ's commands, you'll follow Christ straight to your calling and you'll have developed the strength, grit, and stability along the way to handle it. If you'll cooperate with Christ and do what He tells you to do in keeping with the words of His mouth and the ways of His heart, you're going to find out how much room holiness makes for wildness. If the apostles and early followers of Jesus didn't live wild lives, I'll unpack my hair dryer from my suitcase, kick my feet up on a couch, and work crossword puzzles.

When you give your heart over to the outrageous occupation of the glorious love of God, He will flabbergast your mind with a living breathing 1 Corinthians 2:9.

**What eye did not see and ear did not hear,
and what never entered the human mind—
God prepared this for those who love Him.**

Eight or so years ago, the last of Keith's two grandmothers passed away. Both of them had been privileged to live long lives so the mourning was assuaged by sweet stories and copious smiles. Gathered on the front steps of a small church that day, we hugged out-of-town cousins we hadn't seen in years and acted like we knew relatives we couldn't have placed if our lives depended on it. We talked about how on earth *so and so's* kids could have grown up so fast and how good it was to see *so and so* out of rehab. And we meant it.

In a little while, the front doors opened and we all filed in. We still had a few minutes before the service started so people continued to mill around the pews. The casket was up front with the top half open. A large arrangement of white roses in superfluous greenery was draped over the bottom half. They say that people aren't laid to rest in their shoes but you couldn't swear that by me. I think it's a good idea for the most part but I'm a shoe freak and I've got a pair or two that I wouldn't mind taking with me. Anyway, it's not like our feet will hurt.

Once we entered the sanctuary, the volume-ten greetings on the front steps understandably dropped to level twos, giving way to some proper reverence. Instrumental music was playing politely over the speakers. People began to whisper about how lovely the flowers were and wondering which ones they'd sent and a hush fell over the loud back-patting and the echoing *How you beens.* Then all the sudden—I do mean out of the clear blue—as loud as you have ever heard anybody use an indoor voice, one of Keith's aunts screamed from the front of the sanctuary, "That's not my mother!"

You have never seen a pair of funeral directors jump to attention that expeditiously in your entire life. They leaped pews in single bounds, neckties flying over their heads. I'm pretty sure their hair even moved— or that's the way I remember it. You can imagine the ruckus that broke out. Relatives rushed to the front and those who couldn't push through the crowd craned their necks and said, "Well, is it her or not?"

It was the best funeral I've ever attended.

Finally, the verdict was in. It was Grandma alright. If it hadn't been, I feel like the funeral directors might have collapsed right in her casket with her, polished shoes and all. Then, who in tarnation knows how we ever would have unearthed real Grandma. Everybody sat up good and straight through the service that day, exhilarated, the blood rushing fresh through our veins. Not one person nodded off even through the reading of an obituary that named relatives thrice removed.

Imagine that your service is going just fine. Your obituary is read and the usual nice things are said. Everything is perfectly proper. Even the grandkids are behaving. Two of them are sound asleep. The pianist knows the specials by heart. Over the better part of an hour, the order of service finally narrows down to the closing prayer. Everybody still awake bows their head. Then all the sudden—I do mean out of the clear blue—as loud as you have ever heard anybody use an indoor voice, one of your daughters stands up and screams, "That's not my mother!" Or maybe you don't have kids and it's your niece who stands up and screams, "That's not my aunt!" Or maybe it's somebody who worked for you who stands up and screams, "That's not my boss!" Or maybe it's a student from the high school where you toiled for twenty solid years who screams, "That's not my teacher!"

"I'll tell you about that woman right there!" she says. "That woman was brave and bold and adventurous and had the audacity to love people who didn't even like her. She forgave people and graced people like no one I've ever known. She helped total strangers behind your back. She dared to ask people how they *really* were. She raised money for orphans. She sponsored middle school camp every single summer and slept in a bunk bed in the same unair-conditioned room with thirty twelve-year-olds when she could have been home eating pound cake. That woman in that casket had the courage to face obstacles you can't even believe. In those last months, when she was so sick she couldn't get out of bed, she got somebody from her church to drop by every week with a list of names and needs so she could put her time to good use and pray for them. And she prayed like she thought God was listening, too. You have no idea what that woman was like out of your sight! I don't even know the same woman you've talked about today. This was the bravest person I've ever known."

And it will be the best funeral somebody there ever attended.

Who knows? She might decide she wants one just like it.

The Verve of the Humble Adventure

*V*erve is my new favorite word. I don't know where it's been all my life. I can't remember once saying it out loud or typing it on a screen until writing this book. I even like how you have to plant your top teeth on your bottom lip twice in one quick syllable to say it. Go ahead and try it. Maybe that explains what took me so long. I had the worst buckteeth in the free world in elementary school. In case you think I'm exaggerating, I wore varying degrees of wire on my teeth for twelve solid years. And I still sleep in a retainer. Who does that at my age? Several years ago, I was leaned back in a child-size dental chair with my feet dangling off the end, when my orthodontist told me any time he sees an ad in the Houston paper about a local event where I'm speaking, he points to the promo picture and says, "I know for a fact that woman has an overbite."

The peak reach of my buckteeth occurred in the third grade. I do mean all nine months of it and under the awe-inspiring instruction of Mrs. Jones, the surliest elementary teacher in the history of public education. If *verve* happened to have been a vocabulary word that year, my top teeth were incapable of making sufficient contact with my bottom lip even once, let alone twice in a single syllable. If it popped up on a spelling test, maybe I had such a deep woundedness over not being able to say it that I flatly refused to write it. Maybe this is also why, after considerable counseling at several points in my adult life, I'm still inarguably odd and unfixed. What if it turns out that all my issues boiled down to an inability to pronounce the letter "v" in the third grade? Someone should have billed Mrs. Jones for untold hours of counseling. I feel sure she scared the verve right out of me.

So, today I intend to take it back. We're sparing the time to fixate on the word because it rises to the top in *Webster's* third definition of *audacious*.

au•da•cious \ȯ-ˈdā-shəs\ *adjective*
3: marked by originality and verve[1]

For those of you who also had severe buckteeth, wicked third grade teachers, or equally valid reasons for repressed verve, this is what the word means:

verve \ˈvərv\ *noun*
1 *archaic*: special ability or talent
2 a: the spirit and enthusiasm animating artistic composition or performance: VIVACITY
b: ENERGY, VITALITY[2]

---

1. Frederick C. Mish, ed., *Merriam-Webster's Collegiate Dictionary* (Springfield, MA: Merriam-Webster, Inc., 2003), 80.
2. Ibid.

Enthusiasm, vivacity, energy, vitality. Those are four aerobic synonyms in anybody's dictionary. The fact is it's hard to audaciously love without a whit of animation. I'm not suggesting we have to bounce around on our tails like Tigger but audacity does call for a little vivacity. The good news is, we don't have to rev ourselves up with a daily rant or shout "look alive!" every morning to the mirror. We could start beckoning Jesus to wake us up to a hike with Him that becomes a greater reality than anything we can see with human eyes or touch with human hands.

To grab hold of His unseen robe and hang on tight for the hike of our life, let's turn loose of every trace of the imaginary friend syndrome. You know what I mean: mostly playing like Jesus is there. Saying something to Him and hoping He heard it. Feeling a little silly like we're talking to ourselves but taking the chance in case the Bible is telling the truth. Walking to the car after a church service feeling almost high then pulling out of the parking lot wondering if we're all making this up. We've all done it. We've all treated Jesus like our imaginary friend and as though, if He turns out to be an illusion, at least we were better off safe than sorry. In fact, amid the first flickers of faith, nothing is more natural than taking the all-purpose approach:

God, if You're really out there then . . .

It's damage control in case it's a lie. It's half-hearted, so the other half won't risk proving foolish. And it's totally natural. But you and I aren't pursuing something natural. The sentences of our stories are meant to be penned from the inkwell of the supernatural. We want God to be able to perform wonders in our clay and do the kinds of things with us that He did with His followers back in their day. If we stay wishy-washy, our little faith will see few results and our few results will breed littler faith. By God's sovereign design, faith is the fertilizer in the seedbed where wonders sprout. Jesus said it these two ways:

"Go. As you have believed, let it be done for you." (Matt. 8:13)

And one chapter later,

"Let it be done for you according to your faith!" (Matt. 9:29)

When I was in my early twenties, one of my Sunday school teachers wrapped up a lesson with this summation: "If it turns out to be untrue, it was still a good way to live." In other words, Jesus was still the best bet. So, was hedging our bets what church was about? If so, maybe I'd rather sleep in on Sunday mornings. The statement left me bewildered, replaying it often in my head and wrestling with whether or not to embrace it. Several years later, God stirred up a ferocious appetite in me to study Scripture and all bets were off. I'd never seen anything as brilliant as the Bible. I encountered the One whose warm breath burned words on scrolls and, lo and behold, He took my breath away. Perhaps the same thing happened to my Sunday school teacher. I hope so, because, at some point, if we're really going to do this thing, we must, in the earth-quaking, stone-rolling words of the risen Christ,

"Stop doubting and believe." (John 20:27 NIV)

The Verve of the Humble Adventure

Let's let go of Jesus as our imaginary friend. Let's exercise a fiery faith fed by the facts of Scripture and approach the genuine Him. He's not the conjured-up answer to our need for a crutch. He is God.

The One who can change everything.

The One who can do anything.

The One who is closer to us than our lungs to our ribs, than our joints to our ligaments, than our bones to our muscles, than our muscles to our skin, than our eyes to our lids.

This is God in our immediate midst, ever present, ever able, ever active and no less willing than He's ever been.

God, who is completely acquainted with the roots of all our fears and reasons for all our tears even when we ourselves have no idea why we're crying.

God, who can impart wisdom to us beyond our years and our experiences just because we asked. (James 1:5)

God, who can infuse us with supernatural stamina to climb over insurmountable obstacles and use our very voices to move mountains from here to there.

God, who can gift us beyond any conceivable explanation and accomplish works through us with ramifications that will outlast time.

This is God who can make us feel what we don't.

We are the resting place of this very God's inconceivable favor. What if we awakened to it and took Him up on the animated relationship He's really offering? What if we quit suffocating our spiritual lives like pillows over our faces, being tentative and timid and unsure for the fifteen-thousandth time? What if, instead, we threw caution to the wind, took Him at His word, and fully engaged in a wide-open, chain-breaking, story-making connection?

Then everything would come alive.

Because He is life and, what He invades, He infuses. What He permeates, He activates.

For each of us across the board to embrace audacious loving and living, an enormous myth begs dispelling. The myth is that some of our lives are too lame and unexciting, generic and insignificant to require audacity and to remotely resemble adventure. Followers of Christ have had to face and fight that lie since the earliest days of Christianity[3] but social media has outrageously propagated a ratings mind-set. Rate of comparison naturally coincides with size of community. Our potential comparison ground is measured according to our range of view, whether in person face to face, or through pictures, or descriptive words.

Centuries ago, the typical range of view was primarily limited to an immediate community. Potential competitors were, for the most part, neighbors. As literacy increased, miles tagged onto a reader's range of

---

3. 2 Cor. 10:12

view through books and newspapers. Then, in the developing world, magazines, ads, movies, television shows, and commercials invading everyday life paved an interstate highway through hills and dales of comparison that earlier generations couldn't have fathomed. One click of a server then burgeoned into a range of view that crosses oceans, hopscotches islands, and wraps around the wide girth of Planet Earth.

Social media—which I love, by the way, and hop on every day—came along and offered us the chance to specialize by jam-packing our core range of view with the kinds of people we most admire and most want to emulate. We have the daily privilege to "watch" people do what we want to do and seemingly be who we wish we could be. Think about the long-term toll. At first all the watching inspires and motivates and brings us hope, but after a while, when we feel like our own paths are moving along slower than we wish or screeching to halts at dead ends, we can start feeling defeated. The more exciting their lives look, the lamer we feel. Never mind that the adventures posted on social media are subject to the provocative spin of the poster. I'm just saying our comparison fields have a lot of manure in them.

If we're not evangelizing people out in the African bush or going undercover as a missionary in the Middle East or fighting injustice on a global scale, we figure *who needs verve?* Certainly not people who take Sunday afternoon naps. I'm writing to say that I beg to differ with that. Don't misunderstand me. If God is calling you to a third world country, update your passport and go! If He's calling you to lay your life down in a nation with murderous hostility toward Christ, take courage and do it! If His hand is to your back in the fight against injustice, swing your fists with all your might! But, should He, for now, leave you right where you are, it's because you can live a bold and daring and adventurous life in Jesus Christ while still pulling into a driveway at the same old address.

Not one of us is managing to dodge weakness, loss, heartbreak, betrayal, rejection, uncertainty, apathy, failure, doubt, upheaval, and unbelief right where the soles of our feet have us. In thirty years of travels and countless informal interviews, I have yet to get to know the person getting by easy. Some lives are woefully harder than others but not one of us is escaping every ounce of pain. I know that because, if you were taking enough painkillers to obliterate all your pain, you wouldn't stay coherent long enough to read this chapter. Most of us have people nearby in dire straits, people who need help in the worst way—people who are in crisis, and not in Christ. If we don't, then we need to get in the car, put it in drive, and find them. Whether you work in hotel housekeeping in a town of five thousand or could spend five thousand dollars a night in a 5-Star suite, between your problems and the problems of those around you, your life calls for verve and qualifies as adventure.

Sometimes we just need a little help locating the spot in our personal sphere of activity with the greatest potential for adventure. I can tell you one fail-safe way to find it:

Peruse your own expense report.

I'm not referring to dollars and cents, though a crave for adventure has been known to drain a bank account. I'm talking about personal expenses: the things in your life that really cost you. Adventure and expense often hold hands. Look for one and you'll often find the other. I'll throw a word picture of the apostle Paul on the page to illustrate the point. We're hard-pressed to find anybody on record in the New Testament besides Jesus Himself who lived a more adventurous life and, not coincidentally, no one requested more prayer for boldness. Take a thorough perusal of one list of his escapades told through his own inspired pen.

> *²⁴Five times I received 39 lashes from Jews.*
> *²⁵Three times I was beaten with rods by the Romans.*
> *Once I was stoned by my enemies.*
> *Three times I was shipwrecked.*
> *I have spent a night and a day*
> *in the open sea.*
> *²⁶On frequent journeys, I faced*
> *dangers from rivers,*
> *dangers from robbers,*
> *dangers from my own people,*
> *dangers from the Gentiles,*
> *dangers in the city,*
> *dangers in the open country,*
> *dangers on the sea,*
> *and dangers among false brothers;*
> *²⁷labor and hardship,*
> *many sleepless nights, hunger and thirst,*
> *often without food, cold, and lacking clothing.*
> *²⁸Not to mention other things, there is the daily pressure on me: my*
> *care for all the churches.*[4]

Imagine for a moment that we had the chance to sit around a campfire with Paul for an entire evening and beg him *please, please, please* to tell us about his most daring adventures. He wouldn't share the stops on

---

4. 2 Cor. 11:24–28

his route where he slept on the best mattresses. He wouldn't tell us his five favorite exotic meals, though it pains me to assume that. Paul's story from the mouth of his knife and fork could hold considerable promise. No telling what he ate with the islanders while he was stranded in Malta in the wake of a shipwreck.[5] That's an episode of *Survivor* that maybe we'll see on the really big screen past the pearly gates. But, if the apostle gave us audience for his most daring adventures retold, he'd far more likely clip from the list above or another like it. In 2 Corinthians 11:23, he refers to being *near death many times*. No way would we let him get away without sharing a few of those.

And we'd listen, slack-jawed and spellbound. But amid the fair high of a secondhand adrenaline rush, the stories would be wasted on us if we didn't factor in the cost. Those lashes, rods, and stones hurt. Some of them would have caused permanent injuries. The shipwrecks were scary. The waters were cold. The arrow on his compass seemed to pierce him wherever it took him. The dangers he faced were real and took their toll. Going without sleep for days on end almost drives a person mad. And being hungry? Think how grouchy we are by dinnertime if we missed lunch. And *the daily pressure?*[6] Well, you know about that one, don't you?

Maybe you've been near death many times, too. Most of us have friends and loved ones who have battled diseases that have put them at the brink numerous times. Maybe you've suffered horrendous physical injuries from an accident or, God forbid, a beating. Maybe you've nearly drowned or, like Paul, been overexposed to harsh elements. I hear true stories continually that are more hair-raising than fiction. I stood over the hospital bed of a young woman who was the lone survivor in a carload of missionaries caught in a hailstorm of gunfire in Iraq. Her

5. Acts 28:1–10
6. 2 Cor. 11:28

beloved husband was in that car. She'd sustained a staggering number of wounds but each bullet had miraculously dodged major organs and arteries. Perhaps you've endured something equally traumatic.

But maybe you're just trying to stay afloat in a family shipwreck. Maybe you're nearly freezing to death in an ice-cold relationship. Maybe, in the wording of Paul, you've faced *dangers from [your] own people*. What could be more demoralizing than feeling unsafe and at highest risk among your very own people? Maybe you're a single mom under spine-cracking stress who can't remember your last good night's sleep. Maybe you suffer the lack of something that so many others seem to possess with little effort. Decent health? A spouse? A baby? A job? A good friend? A whole mind? A basic place to live? A woman contacted me yesterday asking for prayer as she faced a twenty-four-hour countdown to homelessness.

Many of our perils are deeply personal and out of public sight. We've each faced situations and circumstances we were not sure we could emotionally survive. We've been treated treacherously and carelessly. Or we've been simply ignored. We've cared for people who ailed for longer than we thought we could endure. We've been the ones to ail, to be forced to depend, and to fear becoming a burden. We've been quiet at times we wanted to scream and we've screamed at times we really wanted to jump. We've ached and pined over the brevity of life and creaked and groaned when it felt unbearably long. We've hung in there when we wanted to quit. We've stayed where we wanted to leave. Been where we wanted to bale. Never underestimate the verve of humble adventures that impress no one but Jesus. These things were costly.

Expensive.

You need to know this very season, this very day, this very moment that Jesus counts the cost. He knows the personal price you're paying. He esteems with especially high regard when your faithfulness to Him is expensive and when you endure or do the right thing solely because you love Him. Read these next words carefully. *He also knows when our unfaithfulness and our fleeing from Him are the very things that cost us dearly.* Boy, have I been there. But something miraculous and gorgeous can happen in the secret spaces of our greatest expenses. We can engage with Jesus there. Fully. Actively. Verbally. We can talk to Him like people who know He really is there. Tell Him what is really going on in our minds, who is frustrating us beyond our last whiff of patience, how tired we are, how mad we are, or, for the love of God, how bored we are. We can fellowship with Him right in the middle of that expensive moment. When we feel stuck or smothered, we can turn that jail cell into the Holy of Holies. We can cry out or moan or just sit in tired silence and think four coherent words: *Jesus, I need You.*

You have Me. Tell Me what you need. Tell Me what you want. Tell Me how you feel. Tell Me how you don't.

We can become alert to His presence, awake and aware of our communion with Him. And we can draw from Him. We can draw bona fide strength from Him, achieving-power, sudden clarity and insight, palpable consolation and comfort. Rest for our weary souls. A breath of calm in our outbreak of anxiety. Energy in our lethargy. We can draw faith for a future that breaks the mirror of our past. We can draw the unction and the wherewithal to resist the temptation to throw something away that we know deep in our hearts we really want to keep.

And that's not all. We can draw joy from Him. Relief. Laughter. We can gulp down hope when a moment is hard to swallow. We can draw buckets from the bottomless well of His love so we have something to give the people in our lives who drain us dry. We can also draw something for ourselves when we've ground our own encouragers to dust.

Jesus is our affluence in affliction. When life gets expensive, take Him up on it. We're living like paupers in a bank vault. The resources are right there because He is right there. And He's listening. Talk to Him. This is not your imaginary friend who gives you imaginary company and imaginary power, both of which vanish into thin air when you return to your right mind. Christ's works have lasting effects and real life applications. No imaginary friend could have done for me what Jesus has managed to do. Even in the black of night when no one is looking, I'm not the same woman I used to be. He alone can rebuild the train wreck that chains of poor decisions have caused. He has performed miracle after miracle in me and around me. Droves of people within miles of our front doors could make the same claims. I don't care if we're junior Steven Spielbergs, we don't have enough imagination to make this stuff up.

We don't have to bite our fingernails to the quick and hope He's there. We can know it well because we know *Him* well. That's how angst became adventure in the life of the apostle Paul. He related to Christ in the ebb and flow of highs and lows as surely as he would have if Christ were constantly visible. *The Lord stood with me and strengthened me.*[7] Paul didn't just think Jesus was real and present and active. He knew He was. In his own words,

> *I know the One I have believed in and am persuaded that He is able to guard what has been entrusted to me until that day.* (2 Tim. 1:12)

I know the One I have believed in. Some adventures take place only between the two of you. That's where powdery faith congeals. Remember

---

7. 2 Tim. 4:17

that third definition of *audacious*? Take another look at it and lock your gaze on the first lovely phrase.

au•da•cious \ȯ-ˈdā-shəs\ *adjective*
3: marked by originality and verve[8]

Problems are common to all of us. Unfortunately, so are losses and disappointments. But, in all the commonality of the human condition, you are exquisitely *un*common. Don't roll your eyes and get cynical on me. We never get so mature or sophisticated that somewhere down in the marrow of our bones we don't still wish we'd turn out to be special. Your own private journey with Jesus through near misses, narrow passages, long nights, and lean days is wholly and completely marked by originality. You may find numerous people who encounter identical struggles, circumstances, or sicknesses but they aren't you as they do. They don't have your DNA. They don't possess your . . .

exact background,

bank account,

family history,

personality,

gift mix,

living environment,

level of sensitivity,

life experience,

and learning style.

They don't mirror your physical traits to the last freckle, birthmark and scar. They don't possess your . . .

---

8. Frederick C. Mish, ed., *Merriam-Webster's Collegiate Dictionary* (Springfield, MA: Merriam-Webster, Inc., 2003), 80.

inherent tendencies,

thought processes,

strengths and weaknesses,

phobias,

frailties,

allergies,

and specialties.

You don't blend into a mortal mush of gray in the sight of God. You aren't conveniently categorized to help God keep His thoughts straight. Have the audacity to believe that this divine adventure of twists and turns is unique to the two of you and marked by originality.

If what you need is a way of escape, Jesus will provide it. He is your inexhaustible provision to abide until He does. No trouble or trial in all its bloody color is a greater reality than this ever-present Savior who has pursued you and wooed you. He, in all His glorious immortality, chose to retain the scars of His flesh-and-blood experience. He bears the marks. He still relates. *"Reach out your hand and put it into My side."*[9]

Rewind the New Testament clock several weeks and you'll find a brief account that opens the twelfth chapter of John. The flashlight moves around the dining room from one individual to another then suddenly lands on a table built for two: Jesus and a woman named Mary from a town called Bethany.

Six days before the Passover, Jesus came to Bethany where Lazarus was, the one Jesus had raised from the dead. So they gave a dinner for Him there; Martha was serving them, and Lazarus was one of those reclining at the table with Him. Then Mary took a pound of fragrant

---

9. John 20:27

oil—pure and expensive nard—anointed Jesus' feet, and wiped His feet with her hair. So the house was filled with the fragrance of the oil. Then one of His disciples, Judas Iscariot (who was about to betray Him), said, "Why wasn't this fragrant oil sold for 300 denarii and given to the poor?" He didn't say this because he cared about the poor but because he was a thief. He was in charge of the money-bag and would steal part of what was put in it.[10]

Did you catch what Mary of Bethany did with something expensive? She drenched the feet of Jesus with it. She didn't dot it or blot it. She gushed it. She poured out every ounce—and not in a puddle on the floor where it would be wasted, but on the feet of Jesus where it would be prized. Judas was appalled, claiming that it could have been put to far better use. That's what thieves do when they see a lost opportunity to steal a profit.

Nobody can tell you what to do with the things that cost you. They are yours. Like every scar, they are part of how you are marked with originality. But you have the right, if you audaciously insist, to pour every last ounce on the feet of Jesus. A Judas of some kind lurks in close proximity to each expensive offering.

"It's too much," he'll say.

"Jesus is not worth it," he'll say.

"He's probably not even who He says," he'll say.

"Look what He's let you go through," he'll say.

"You can put this to much better use," he'll say.

"You will look like a fool to your people," he'll say.

---

10. John 12:1–6

He's a thief. He's trying to steal this from you to rob the redemption and profit the darkness. If you've got enough nerve and verve, you might consider saying just one little word back to him.

Move.

It's entirely your call but, should you take what's expensive and lavish it on the feet of Jesus, there, just beyond the mortal senses, your house—
   or your workplace,
   your hospital room,
   your mobile home,
   your dorm room,
   your church sanctuary,
   or your prison cell
—will be filled with the fragrant scent of Earth's most precious oil.

Need Is Not Enough

Picture a world where people actually do what they need to do. A teenage girl glances back at her bedroom right as she walks out the door to head for school. She sees the fourteen outfits strewn around the room that she'd tried on and rejected. One of them is draped over the lampshade and two others are hanging from the blades of her ceiling fan. She suddenly thinks to herself, *I really need to clean my room!* She throws down her books, pitches her purse, trips over three pair of shoes on the way to her closet, and she starts grabbing coat hangers. On her way out the front door, she sees her mother putting organic cereal boxes back on the shelf and thinks, *I need to help my mom or she's going to be late to work.* She dashes to the sink with the speed of lightning, rinses the goji berries and chia seeds out of the cereal bowls, and sets them in the dishwasher. She fills the small compartment with high efficiency detergent, shuts the dishwasher door, and selects *energy saver.* She needs to hug her mom so, of course, she does—but then she flies out the door because she needs to get to school before the 8:00 a.m. bell rings.

Heaven on earth.

It's Sunday morning and you think to yourself, *I need to go to church today* so you make haste, take a water-economizing shower, and get dressed. When you glance in the mirror, you realize that your skirt is the tiniest tad tighter than it was the last time you wore it. "I need to exercise!" Why not multitask? So, you strap on your ankle weights and wear them to church. You can't find a parking place within blocks of the building but you need to walk anyway. So, you do. It's a hot humid morning and the ankle weights are making you sweat like a saddled horse but you read somewhere that the human body needs to sweat so you choose to feel gratified that your hair is now matted to your scalp. Your friends are going to Chili's after the service and you really want to go, but the pastor brought up the effectiveness of fasting in the third point of his sermon. You tell them you'd like to go but you need to fast. They're aghast. "We need to, too!" And they do. So no one goes to lunch. But no one's upset because they live in a world where people do what they need to do.

Just imagine what life would be like.

"I need to change." Poof. I change.

"I need to go to the store." Off I go.

"I need to be a better friend." Two hours on the phone and by noon I am.

"I need a haircut." Grab the kitchen shears. Who really needs to go to a salon if she owns a pair of scissors? If she likes tapered ends, she can use a bread knife.

"I need a drink." Whoops. Back up. "I need a drink of water." That's better. In fact, some experts say you need an ounce for every pound you weigh, so jump on the scale and guzzle down accordingly. Make that vitamin water.

While changing your antimicrobial bed sheets, you catch a glimpse of your neighbor running past your house in her black and purple spandex. "I need to run, too!" By now the blisters from the ankle weights you wore to church have calloused over. You grab your biodegradable athletic footwear and out you go, but soon, in you come, taking short, quick steps on your tiptoes because what you really need is to go to the restroom. All that vitamin water.

A reminder pops up on a man's smart phone. He jumps to his feet from the chair in the den where he's been watching a documentary on sound financial planning. He finds his wife who is darning socks, stands her to her feet in her orthopedic Toms, plants a kiss on her SPF 30 hydrated lips, then he affirms her seven times while looking her in the eyes. Next he needs to hug his children. He finds his school-age children in their clean rooms doing their homework for extra credit and his two-year-old little boy red-faced on the potty seat.

If we lived in a world where people actually did what they need to do, nobody with any money would run out of gas, nobody would get a speeding ticket, nobody would miss jury duty, nobody would be excessive, nobody would get a root canal, nobody would get grounded, nobody would take fiber supplements, and nobody but nobody would drink *Dr. Pepper.* Drug rehabs would be dinosaurs and *AA* would stand for Admittedly Admirable.

So, why on earth don't we all just do what we need to do? If we did, we'd all be, come to think of it, *practically perfect.* Eve never would've reached for that tree and the serpent would've lacked a target to deceive. It seems like God would have just made us that way and saved Himself the considerable trouble of saving us.

All this need reminds me of my mother. She was one of the quirkiest people I've ever had the pleasure to know. Only my daughters amuse me like she did. Quick witted and well read, she was the fastest draw with a comeback this side of the Mississippi. She preferred cigarettes to exercise to maintain her weight, but if she had her druthers, she would not be caught dead in the act of purchasing them. That was my Dad's job, one pack of L&Ms at a time. Mind you, he hadn't smoked since World War II and the smell of tobacco tended to trip his gag reflex.

Mom preferred instant coffee to brewed, plastic forks to stainless, and she only used pancake mix labeled *just add water*. She never closed a book without opening up another and had a working vocabulary that could've made Noah Webster sing and spin in circles to the "Hallelujah Chorus." That said, ask any of us five kids, and we will testify that the most oft-repeated words that fell from our mother's lips were these: "I need to go to the grocery store."

She almost never did. She'd do anything to avoid it including washing off leftover frozen Swedish meatballs and reheating them on the stove with a jar of Ragu. Setting aside holidays when she could whip up an impressive pan of cornbread dressing, fancy eating at my mother's house was a Salisbury steak frozen dinner. I got to where I liked them. Somehow her sublime company made up for the translucent mashed potatoes. We had "Queen of Everything" etched on her grave marker because, to us, she was. We adored her. But we regretted that we never talked her into writing a cookbook called *How to Feed a Family of Eight without Going to the Grocery Store*. She could have made a fortune and saved all the stamp money she spent on Publishers Clearing House.

The fact is, we don't always do what we need to do. And here is the primary reason: *because we don't want to.*

Generally speaking, when it comes to humankind, want trumps need except in matters of survival. That's what this chapter is all about. We eat and sleep and call 911 in emergencies because we need to stay alive, but we mortal-sorts are compulsively resistant to what we *need* to do to thrive. We know it's a poor trait. We've gotten into terrible trouble over it—as early as the Garden—but something in us bristles at the thought of doing what we need to do for need's sake alone. At the end of the day in the land of the free, people tend to do what they want.

Take, for instance, how great that friendship was going until she told you that she really, really needed you and got that look in her eye like she really, really meant it at a really, really deep level. In that same conversation, she tells you she's a one-friend kind of person. "That's all I really *need*," she says. By the sixteenth text you get the next day at work, you started scratching at hives on the back of your neck and then you start pulling away. Or maybe it's just me. We hate ourselves for it, because we know it's wrong, and we repent because we know it's right. But somehow, in our deeply flawed humanness, that ballooning level of need crowds out the want.

On the other hand, maybe we're nicer people than that. Maybe that's not us in our relationships. It's just us in our refrigerators. There's nothing like needing to go nondairy to make us pull out the Velveeta. When I tell myself I need to eat less salt, all I can think about is that jar of pimento-stuffed olives staring all red and beady-eyed at me from the refrigerator shelf between the dill pickles and the soy sauce. I'm not proud of it. I need to change but that's the whole problem. I don't want to.

Make no mistake. If we really do, no joke, resist everything we need to do, our lives—our relationships, our marriages, our health, our educational pursuits, our houses, our apartments, our cars, our finances—will fall completely apart. We will find ourselves utterly and desolately alone. Nobody is left more wanting than the one who did only what he wanted.

We need need. Need is what saves our scrawny necks when our wants go awry. It's the food of fidelity in a season of fierce temptation. In Ephesians 6:13–17, Paul documents the armor of God that protects a believer in vicious battles with demonic powers. Each piece of armor corresponds theologically with its specific placement on the warrior. The breastplate of righteousness very pointedly and strategically covers and shields the heart. It represents the immense protection that comes from doing the right thing even when we feel the wrong thing.

So, need is good. Desperation is even better, because desperation can change what we need into what we want. That's what happened to me but more on that later. *Hitting bottom* is the term an alcoholic might call the process of descending dramatically from need (*I need to stop drinking*) to desperation (*If I don't stop, this is going to destroy me*). Anyone living in recovery from substance addiction will tell you that sobriety had to become something they deeply wanted and not just deeply needed.

In the ring between competitors for the heavyweight human motivator, want beats need to a bloody pulp. This competition comes into full play nowhere more dramatically than in the ring of our spirituality. Not one of us will get to the end of this book and voraciously keep seeking an audacious love for Jesus because it's what we need to do. When push comes to shove, our driving force will be desire or this will turn out to be just another phase we went through for a week or two. Discipline won't do this for us. Discipline can make us more Christlike but it cannot make us love Christ more. We will never love Him just because we need to. We will only love Him audaciously because we want to.

The first recorded words of Jesus in the NIV's translation of the Gospel of John are immensely relevant to us at this juncture toward divine audacity. You'll find them tucked carefully into this succinct context:

> *The next day John was there again with two of his disciples. When he saw Jesus passing by, he said, "Look, the Lamb of God!" When the two disciples heard him say this, they followed Jesus. Turning around, Jesus saw them following and asked, "What do you want?"*

They said, "Rabbi" (which means "Teacher"), "where are you stay-
ing?" "Come," he replied, "and you will see." (John 1:35–39)

If we were looking at a red-letter edition of the Bible that colors every statement out of the mouth of Christ, this question would be the first splash of red in the Gospel of John:

"What do you want?"

We're apt to assign it an insolent tone because we most commonly hear one in our current culture, but peel that imposition off this ancient context. Jesus simply asked them what they'd come to Him seeking. *Desiring.* Why exactly were they following Him? Not a bad inquiry for us either. It makes us think—and thinking is good. The question is particularly poignant in a Gospel that narrows to a close with another question painted in crimson on the sacred page:

"Do you love Me?"

The bright red bookends of the book of John: *Want. Love.* Jesus made no bones about it: His followers were being invited into a journey of the heart. Stale, sedate religion was *outside-in.* Jesus had come to turn spirituality *inside-out.* He inaugurated an era in which followers would become *Christ's letter . . . not written with ink but with the Spirit of the living God—not on stone tablets but on tablets that are hearts of flesh* (2 Cor. 3:3).

Here's the thing. Jesus is not needy. So, I'm not sure He gets all charged up when this is what He continually hears from our dutiful mouths:

I need to read my Bible.
I need to pray.
I need to go to church.
I need to serve somebody.
I need to give to the poor.
I need to help some people.

And I do. You'd probably say that you do, too. But suppose He'd occasionally like to counter with the same question He presented to the first two people He caught close to His heels:

*What do you **want**?*

Maybe, for the sake of stirring up some thought and turning over some soil where lively relationships get planted and grown, He'd like on occasion to say something resembling this:

I hear what you're saying you need to do and that's good. That's important. That's conviction. That's godly. But this is what I'd really like to hear you respond to: What is it you want? What drives your heart? What exactly has you at My heels? What are you seeking? What are you really looking for? Because this is where we'll find your affections . . .

"For where your treasure is, there your heart will be also."
(Matt. 6:21)

We each get the privilege to grow and to process. We don't just arrive. We get to enjoy the ride with Jesus on a landscape where the scenery is never wasted and every mile counts. But, somewhere along the path of knowing Him and being intrigued by Him and smitten with Him, I think Jesus is looking to hear His all-time-favorite, best-ever answer to the question before His follower.

What do you want?

I WANT YOU. *You,* Jesus. You are what I want most in this entire world.

For the eyes of Yahweh roam throughout the earth to show Himself strong for those whose hearts are completely His (2 Chron. 16:9). Since Jesus reads the heart beneath our words, He's not looking to hear that kind of answer a moment before it is true, but this is a glorious place where authentic desire can take root and begin to grow:

(Your name/my name), what do you want?

Jesus, I want to want YOU. Would You help me?
I already know I need You. But I want to want You, too.

We were created out of divine desire for divine desire. God did not fashion us from the dust because He needed us. He created us because He wanted us. One of the first concepts we hear anything about in our early discipleship as followers of Christ is the call on our lives to do *God's will*. It's Christianity 101. Over and over in His earthly tenure, Jesus talked about having come to earth to do His Father's *will*. Repeatedly in the New Testament, His followers are called to do likewise. If we view God's faithfulness to us and our faithfulness to Him as nothing more than mutual obligation, we will drop out of the loop of soul-satisfaction. God is not asking us to put our hearts out there while He withholds His. God's will is driven by His desire. I hope to prove that to you but I'll need your patience through a quick word study.

The Greek term that most often translates into the noun form of the word *will* in the New Testament is *thelema*. Take a look at two definitions of this term from a couple of Greek dictionaries:

> *that which is desired or wished for*[1]
>
> > *Will, not to be conceived as a demand, but as an expression or inclination of pleasure towards that which is liked, that which pleases and creates joy. When it denotes God's will, it signifies His gracious disposition toward something. Used to designate what God Himself does of His own good pleasure.*[2]

Did you catch these words? *Desire. Pleasure. That which is liked . . . pleases . . . creates joy.* There is nothing cold about the will of God. Nothing plastic, nothing detached. Nothing egomaniacal. Nothing particularly

---

1. J. P. Louw and Eugene A. Nida, *Greek-English Lexicon of the New Testament: Based on Semantic Domains* (New York: United Bible Societies, 1996).
2. Spiros Zodhiates, *The Complete Word Study Dictionary: New Testament* (Chattanooga, TN: AMG Publishers, 2000).

even economical. Thrifty is not what you'd call God. He's lavish by nature, the last to pinch grace like a penny. God's will *for* us and *toward* us doesn't just come from mental calculations. It flows as surely from holy affections. We have been created and called according to His will. He who desires us longs for us to desire Him. That's the way of true love. It is both unselfish and insatiable.

John 17 records the stunningly intimate requests Christ made of His Father on behalf of His followers—both present and future—just minutes before His arrest. Pull out a thermometer from your medicine cabinet and take the temperature on His heart in every line of this excerpt from that twenty-six-verse prayer. Picture Jesus knowing exactly what awaited Him that very night and the next brutal day.

> *20I pray not only for these,*
> *but also for those who believe in Me*
> *through their message.* (Side note: that includes you and me.)
> *21May they all be one,*
> *as You, Father, are in Me and I am in You.*
> *May they also be one in Us,*
> *so the world may believe You sent Me.*
> *22I have given them the glory You have given Me.*
> *May they be one as We are one.*
> *23I am in them and You are in Me.*
> *May they be made completely one,*
> *so the world may know You have sent Me*
> *and have loved them as You have loved Me.*

*²⁴Father, I desire those You have given Me
to be with Me where I am.*³

Does holiness get more intimately and utterly involved than this? *I am in them and You are in Me . . . [You] have loved them as You have loved Me.* Try your best to extend your hands to the immeasurable limits of that bold statement. The Father loves you as He loves His only begotten Son. That's why we can make the claim that God loves each of us, in the words of Augustine, "as if there were only one of us." That's a long, long way from finding you vaguely tolerable and letting you slip unnoticed on a group pass through the door of heaven.

After you've held that one to your chest for a moment, step with both feet on the force of the last verse: *Father, I desire those You have given me to be with Me where I am.* The word *desire* in the verse is translated from the Greek verb *thelo.* You can see from its similarity to *thelema* that the terms spring from the same well of affection.

I'm not sure the human heart has any greater longing than to be desired—and not for just a night but for a lifetime. As surely as an ocean reflects the rising sun, this unearthly longing is a shimmering reflection of *imago Dei.* We don't yearn to be desired solely out of insecurity. We were fashioned with a longing to be wanted so that we would search and find the One who desires us most of all. The Maker of heaven and earth did not create us with desire in order to quash it. He crafted us to captivate and fascinate us and set us ablaze with holy fire.

The Bridegroom, by whom and for whom our hearts were shaped, delights over those with the audacity to take these words from Song of Songs personally, passionately, and prophetically:

---

3. John 17:20–24

I belong to my love and his desire is for me. (7:10)

Try starting your day with that every morning. Look at that woman in the bathroom mirror who wonders if she possesses anything worth wanting and say those words out loud to her. Say them like you mean them. And if, for whatever reason, you need the verse in the worst way—whether over loneliness, loss, abandonment, or rejection—write it on an index card and tape it to the edge of your mirror where you can see it every time you see yourself.

Now, let's flip that index card to the other side. Each page of this book is devoted to the unabashed pursuit of an audacious affection for Jesus that answers His for us. In the reversal of Song of Songs 7:10, I think He longs to say of you and of me,

Her desire is for Me.

Is it even possible for a human to have that kind of desire for an unseen Savior? If invaded by the Holy Spirit of the living God, the answer is a million times yes. This echoing passion is the supreme theme that moved God Himself to call David a man after His own heart. Take David's pulse in Psalm 27:4:

I have asked one thing from the LORD;
it is what I desire:
to dwell in the house of the LORD
all the days of my life,
gazing on the beauty of the LORD.[4]

---

4. Ps. 27:4

Asaph, another psalmist, penned these gorgeous lines:

> [25]*Who do I have in heaven but You?*
> *And I desire nothing on earth but You.*
> [26]*My flesh and my heart may fail,*
> *but God is the strength of my heart,*
> *my portion forever.*[5]

When I first began to fall in love with Christ and crumple the edges of my tidy Bible, I tumbled in all my page-turning to five simple words in Philippians that stole my heart.

I want to know Christ. (Phil. 3:10 NIV)

I do, too! I thought to myself. *Or, at least, I want to want to!* I'd already tail-spun into the ditch numerous times. I knew I *needed* to know Christ. I'd known it for years but that clear fact didn't have the power to glue my face to the page when the desperation passed. One thing alone possessed the force to keep me in it: *I want to know Christ.* The game changer for me was coming to a place where I *wanted* to love Him and I *wanted* to seek Him and I *wanted* to serve Him and I *wanted* to get up before the sun and talk to Him. I was too afraid of missing something meaningful or fascinating or fabulous that He might want to show me or tell me. The miracle of God is that, all these years later, I still felt the same way this morning.

---

5. Ps. 73:25–26

What I needed to do never stuck with me long once I slipped out from under the pressure. It simply wasn't enough to sustain me. My life would ultimately be driven by the same thing as yours: *desire.*

We've come to this point in our trek to audacity to let Jesus ask us the same truth-surfacing, charade-slaying question to prepare us for what's left of our journey:

What do you [really, really, really] want?

Maybe you can already answer that question with the loudest *You, Jesus!* that a mortal mouth has ever shouted. If so, He has won your heart in this present season and you can kick up some dust in boisterous celebration. There's no breakthrough like that breakthrough. But, if, perchance, your face would turn crimson to answer that one question candidly, I just want you to know that I get it. That was me. And that's our next chapter.

A Brand New Want To

My earliest memory kicks in around four years old, spinning on a burlap bag-swing hung from a rope knotted around the bicep of an Arkansas pine. I'd twist the fraying rope as tightly as I could, jump on the bag, hold on for dear life and lean my head back while the swing spun wildly in circles. The goal was to keep my eyes open and watch those pine needles turn into a dizzy blur of feltish green. I'd climb off of that bag and stumble around drunker than Cooter Brown. For a minute or two, I'd feel like throwing up and why that didn't deter me, I'll never know. I just had a thing for that swing. In the summertime when I'd wear shorts, the insides of my skinny thighs would nearly be sanded raw from clamping tight to the burlap. If I had enough chigger bites, I noticed less.

My family moved to Houston while I was in high school but the green hills and good people of Arkansas had already engraved marks on my heart too deep to undo. In all these years, I've never been able to shake my thick accent despite considerable teasing and enduring countless public impersonations. Some of them were pretty good but, frankly, they just did not have the right hair to pull it off. We're all package deals. If you can rock the accent but can't rock the hair, then it's all talk.

Like most regions where the culture runs rich, our colloquialisms were as buttery thick as our accents. Some of our figures of speech were classic Arkansan, others broadly Southern, and still others were by-products of being raised among my wonderful and peculiar kin with deliciously rural roots. I'll say right up front that I don't know which figures of speech came from which of those three origins, so don't go blaming the state of Arkansas for the state of my vocabulary.

Take Cooter Brown, for instance. I have no idea who Cooter Brown was or why he felt the need to drink so much that everybody who did likewise was compared to him. As far as I could tell, Cooter Brown had never been sober for a day of his life. God love him. The issue may have been Mrs. Brown. I just don't know. The only shiny spot on Mr. Brown's dull forehead is that apparently somebody was always drunker. I also do not know if the Browns came from anywhere near my great state but they surely did not come from my hometown because my town was nestled in the ample bosom of a dry county. If Brown wanted to get drunk, he was going to have to drive to Hot Springs to do it.

Several of my family's sayings are firmly lodged in my ongoing vocabulary and I make good use of them multiple times a week. "Stoved-up" is one of them. That means your muscles feel really stiff. I'm not usually referring to myself. I'm ordinarily talking about my border collie, Queen Esther. She does a lot of romping in these woods where Keith and I live and sometimes at the end of the day she is fairly stoved-up. Big Pops, Keith's Daddy, is often stoved-up as well. You always say it just like that. It's always past tense.

Another saying we have is a knock off of the word *dubious*, although, rocket scientist that I am, I did not make the connection until recent years. We pronounce it "DOO-bus" and we use it in sentences like the one my youngest daughter said only last night in my kitchen: "I heard (*so and so happened*) but I'm doobus about it." That means she's finding something fishy about it. Suspicious. Something's not adding up. The Texas Moores have fully embraced my Arkansas dubiosity and say the word continually. And they're better off for it. No other word will suffice in certain contexts. Frankly, there's too much in this world to be doobus about.

"Kindly daffy" is said a good deal around here as well in loving memory of my grandmother, Minnie Ola, who, as far as I know, may well have coined the pairing. It means that a person is pretty well off her rocker (Kindly = "kind of"). In this day and age, there is no end to the opportunities to use this uniquely descriptive term especially if you spend time on the World Wide Web. If my grandmother happened to possess a particular fondness for the person in question, she'd stop short of daffy and simply say, "Poor thing, she just ain't at herself." For instance, had she lived to see a certain spell of my thirties, she would have bemoaned my humble estate with those very words.

My people used the word "swannee" instead of "swear" as in "Well, I swannee, that was the worst sermon I ever heard." If you weren't from our neck of the woods, you were from "sommers else." If you were in a bad mood, you could get glad in the same clothes you got mad in. If you did something stupid, you didn't have a lick of sense and nobody minded letting you know. Where I come from people didn't just cry. They cried in their buttermilk. Don't ask me why. These are questions with answers from the great deep.

I'm bringing all of this up to give you a firm foundation for grasping one of my Daddy's go-to statements. God rest his soul, he died exactly eight years ago today at eighty-six with his travel atlas and Scrabble board wide open on his breakfast table. What he had to say is noteworthy even if for no other reason than he, too, was born in a town called Bethlehem. His father and his father's father are laid to rest in that very community cemetery. Dad's Bethlehem was in Arkansas instead of Judea, but why split hairs? Both had stables and neither had a decent motel.

Any time my Daddy was exasperated, he'd get a certain look on his face, drop his hands to his side and say (emphatically and slowly, about at the pace you'd shoot BBs),

"Well, that just makes me want a dip of snuff."

His own maternal grandmother, Miss Ruthie, did indeed dip snuff—a sight I found decidedly disturbing as a child so I was never sure if my Daddy was not going to make good on his threats. Someone should pass a law prohibiting grown-ups from pressuring little kids to give hello and good-bye kisses to unfathomably aged (two syllables please) great-grandmothers who are, at that very moment, snuff-dipping. For starters, you could accidentally kick over the spitting jug and that right there will maim you for life.

As far as I know, my Daddy never did award himself a dip of snuff but, till his dying day, he took every aggravation as an opportunity to declare that he sure wanted one.

I'm writing to you today to say that I would've had a considerably easier time if all I'd wanted was a dip of snuff. What I wanted was to be wanted and at all costs. What I wanted was for someone to do me wrong and prove that I was right about myself. What I wanted was someone as messed up as me so he'd be less likely to see. I craved security but sabotaged it repeatedly by surrounding myself with relationships and situations that would constantly trip the switches of my endless insecurities.

I was driven by something even more urgent than wave currents of fear. I was driven by panic. My big brother once told me that, when I was a little girl, I always had a look on my face like somebody had just jumped out from behind a black curtain and yelled, "Boo!" Go figure that. I was terrified to be alone, but too scared to be my real self when I wasn't. I had no earthly idea who I was. My identity was based solely on the one I was with. I had to be somebody's something at all times. My own merit had no merit. I was only worth what I saw reflected in another person's eyes. I was a field with no fence and, had my life been a Webster's, the word "no" would have been missing entirely between "nix" and "no-account."

I wanted to be wanted so badly that I'd adhere myself to people I didn't even like as long as they liked me. *Please love me. I can make you love me. I can make you happy.* People would have called me an agreeable sort. *Where do you want to eat, Beth? Anywhere you do. What do you want to do, Beth? Anything you do. Just stay with me. Want me. Love me.* Here's the biggest one: *Take care of me.* In a way I find completely baffling today, I was utterly convinced in my earlier years that I could not take care of myself. The irony is that I always ended up being the caretaker. Apparently, I could take care of anybody but me. I could tell you stories and situations from my childhood and adolescence that could help you understand why I came out that way, but who but God knows if I would have been a clot of tangled nerves anyway?

I had a side that was glad to be bad. I felt destined for it. Resigned to it. I have a startlingly clear memory of being fourteen years old—never having sipped a beer or smoked a joint—wondering what my personal drug of choice would end up being. At the very same time, I also wanted to be a good girl in the worst way and often pretended I was one. Little girls who have been sexually abused and forced to keep terrible secrets learn early on how to get their game on. I played that game, first string, all the way from elementary school to middle school and on to three different high schools, then packed up my game gear after graduation and moved it straight into my college dorm room.

Looking back on those years, I've often wondered if it's still called hypocrisy if the person you're pretending to be is the one you really wish you could be. Thank God, He looks on the heart, seeing straight through our pretense to our pain. When He looked on my heart, He saw one malformed, malnourished, malfunctioning mess. My whole life was a bloody fight for wanting things that can't coexist.

The long and short of it is, our wants can be really messed up. And, if they are, our lives will be really messed up because we humans, except in matters of survival, are driven most by what we desire. We can want things desperately, clawing and clamoring, that we know have the capacity to destroy us. The gratification of desire is so strong that we, with our eyes wide open, are willing to satisfy it today even if we dearly pay for ten thousand tomorrows.

The heart is more deceitful than anything else.

That's what Jeremiah 17:9 says. It will lie like a dog. It can make you think you're going to live happily ever after with a guy who hasn't been happy a single day since you met him. It can make you chase a dream of fame until it turns into your worst nightmare. It says that how you feel right now is how you'll feel forever. It argues that life is not worth the effort and your family would be better off without you. A deceptive heart can convince you that you were meant for somebody else's husband and that thirty minutes of wonderful is worth three decades of regret. It can tell you that, if you're stealing from your company to do more for your children, it's okay. You'll pay it back as soon as you get some overtime. *Good grief,* a lying heart says, *the company is stealing from you anyway by not paying you what you're worth. They owe this to you.*

A deceitful heart can rationalize that God still gets great glory from a great story you've mostly made up. *Look how people are being touched by it.* A deceitful heart says, *If I really want it, God must mean for me to have it.* And, *God made me this way. It's the way I'm wired.* It says that going to church means you're going to heaven. It can tell you that there's no real harm in pornography because nobody's getting hurt and prostitution is victimless so who really cares? It insists that all is fair in love and war and the end justifies the means and what you don't know can't hurt you. It says that fire won't burn you, ice won't freeze you, and quicksand won't swallow you whole. It promises you that you're not the kind to get addicted. *I can stop any time I want.* In the infamous words of Samson, *I will go out as at other times and shake myself free.* But that was exactly the time he couldn't. It says that being with somebody, no matter how destructive or dysfunctional, always beat being alone and, if enough money is in it, you can put up with anything.

Until you can't.

There once was a man named Solomon. Study his ways before you follow him. He, too, thought that, if he could just have everything his human heart desired, he'd be happy. Turned out, he wasn't.

⁸I also amassed silver and gold for myself, and the treasure of kings and provinces. I gathered male and female singers for myself, and many concubines, the delights of men. ⁹So I became great and surpassed all who were before me in Jerusalem; my wisdom also remained with me. ¹⁰All that my eyes desired, I did not deny them. I did not refuse myself any pleasure, for I took pleasure in all my struggles. This was my reward for all my struggles. ¹¹When I considered all that I had accomplished and what I had labored to achieve, I found everything to be futile and a pursuit of the wind. There was nothing to be gained under the sun.[1]

Nothing is more depressing than realizing that we no longer want what we always wanted once we finally have it. No death feels deader than the death of desire. If we don't know what we want, we don't know who we are. That's when some of us finally slink over to Jesus because, if we're going to be dead to desire anyway, we figure we might as well be religious. What else do we have to lose? The fact that Jesus is willing to show up in beauty where we'd surrendered to duty is a testament to His jaw-dropping grace. He'll put up with any motive if it will stick us on the path where we'll bump into His presence. And, once we do, we might decide, since we have nothing else to lose, to lose ourselves in Him.

But then something completely unexpected happens. He awakens desire. He calls it forth from the dead and starts unwinding its binding and sending it twirling like a little girl in an A-line skirt. You start feeling more than you've ever felt in your life. But, oddly, these aren't the old desires. It's not that they're nowhere in there. It's that they're squashed by something weightier and shushed by something louder and paled by something brighter. Something new is happening. You're no longer out to destroy yourself by feeding your flesh so fat that it suffocates your spirit. You no longer love yourself into hating yourself.

Desperation can do the same thing if it leads us to collapse in a heap at the feet of Jesus. Life becomes so excruciating that we finally want what we need. In that precise surrender we discover that what we

---

1. Eccles. 2:8–11

need is what we want more than anything else in this world. Next to the redemption of our very souls, nothing is more glorious and miraculous than the redemption of our desires. Never think for a moment that Jesus cannot heal a messed up heart. It is His forte. His *métier*. Sweep up every scattered shard of your heart into one huge dustpan and dump it entirely into His palms. He will draw a deep breath, blow away the dirt, and refashion what remains, piece by piece, into a mosaic of startling beauty and sufficient humility to hold something utterly splendid.

It's the authentic that exposes the counterfeit. We fall out of a lesser love by falling into one greater. We quit trying to warm ourselves by the wick of a candle when we learn what it's like to stretch ourselves out in the noonday sun. We don't know what we're missing with our box fans until we take off our scarves and stand in howling holy wind. Life-breathing love is the only thing lethal enough to kill murderous desire.

Stare at the prospect of your future through the lens of this promise:

Take delight in the LORD, and He will give you your heart's desires.
(Ps. 37:4)

How can the psalmist place such a bold, across-the-board claim on the thorny grass of a lusty world? Inside-out delight in God drives so much dross out of the heart that we can dare to trust what we feel. The desires that can dwell and propagate under the roof of divine delight are those God can bless with unleashed glee. You see, desire is not the problem. We were created for it. Deceit is the problem and it draws to a heart of flesh like iron filings to a magnet. Only one thing has the power to extract thorns of deceit from the hominess they find in a human heart: truth. *Christ's truth*. In His own words,

"You will know the truth and the truth will set you free." (John 8:32)

We have to know it, get it down in our bones, and stuffed into our belief systems until it's breaking threads and popping through the seams. We don't just pat the Truth occasionally on our bedside tables or settle for feeling good about our Holy Bible cell phone app. We plant our faces in the pages. There to that immutable Truth we bring what's true about us. We drag every want into the light whether it's wrong or undeniably right. We bring each ache and every sigh and every *"how long, O Lord?"* into His knowing presence without fear of rejection, revulsion or reprisal.

Lord, my every desire is known to You;
my sighing is not hidden from You. (Ps. 38:9)

A healthy heart spreads every desire on the open table of divine dialogue.

This is what I long for, Lord . . .

And when we know those desires are wrong or toxic, we talk them out with equal liberty and try to identify the bed of need beneath the body of craving. Often when I'm pouring my heart out to God aloud, I will hear my mouth say what my thoughts alone could never articulate. Freedom of speech is the flooring invitation that is taped like a birthday card to the gift of our salvation. Jesus sits at the right hand of God interceding for us as one who has been tempted in every conceivable way. There in His presence, we get to *be* ourselves, not just *behave* ourselves. We're not bound and gagged. We're loosed and heard.

When we're red-faced over what we find our hearts are longing for, we bring it out in the open before Him instead of holding it inside where it incubates in warm, dark secret and hatches into action. Freedom is telling God what we desperately want. Trust is asking Him to change our want if gaining it would poison us. We don't just sit back and stare into our empty hands. We open them up, stretch them out, and ask Him to fill them with something better.

> *Increase my delight in You so that my desires start sifting and shifting until they align with the ones You hold tightly in Your hand for me. Your desire is to profusely bless me, not withhold from me. You are trustworthy. You will never respond to my full surrender by starving my soul and leaving me empty. Give me the wants You want because anything less will rob me.*

Something otherworldly erupts within us and washes over us when we start wanting what the Spirit of God wants. Call it the anointing. We start experiencing the abundance of John 10:10[2] that many can quote but none can adequately describe to us. Spiritual gifts that had barely surfaced begin surging. This odd joy starts stirring within us. We laugh a little more and worry a little less because *the mind-set of the Spirit is life and peace* (Rom. 8:6). We start liking people we could not stand. Some of them will think we're freaks but they'll tell us on occasion that they feel different around us, like maybe life's not such a living hell. Our lives begin bearing obvious fruit and others are affected and blessed and built up by God and no one is more surprised than we are. We still meet hardships and difficulties and disappointments and losses but not as those

---

2. "A thief comes only to steal and to kill and to destroy. I have come so that they may have life and have it in abundance" (John 10:10).

without hope, not as those without purpose, and not as those without power. Life is still work but, bless God, it works.

> *For it is God who is working in you, enabling you both to desire and to work out His good purpose.* (Phil. 2:13)

It will never be rules that most effectively deter us from jumping headlong into sin. In the wording of Colossians 2:21, regulations like *Do not handle, Do not taste, Do not touch* don't cut it. *These have indeed an appearance of wisdom in promoting self-made religion and asceticism and severity to the body, but they are of no value in stopping the indulgence of the flesh* (Col. 2:23 ESV).

Here's what most effectively diminishes our indulgence in the flesh: our indulgence in the Spirit. *Christ's Spirit.*[3] By all means, indulge. In fact, do it *Merriam-Webster's* way.

> **in•dulge** \in-'dəlj\ *verb*
> *1 a:* to give free rein to
> *b:* to take unrestrained pleasure in: GRATIFY[4]

Go right ahead. Be His guest. Give free rein to Him. Take unrestrained pleasure in Him. There's no end to Jesus. No way to wear Him out. No way to plug the spring and make the well run dry. No way to end up in a colossal codependent mess. He's just not one to co-depend. To love Him first is to love others best. You can't win Him and lose nor lose Him and win. Without Him, everything else is . . . well, a dip of

---

3. Rom. 8:9
4. Frederick C. Mish, ed., *Merriam-Webster's Collegiate Dictionary* (Springfield, MA: Merriam-Webster, Inc., 2003), 637.

snuff. You may think you want it but sooner or later you'll have to find somewhere to spit it.

As long as we're walking around in these suits of porous skin and breathing a fallen world's polluted air, we'll have desires pop up in our hearts that come from our carnal natures or what Scripture calls our flesh.[5] Sometimes we'll stand firm and other times we'll quench the Holy Spirit and go with those desires and dip all kinds of snuff.

But here's what I'm telling you: Once we've been caught up in the delight of divine desire, we will never be satisfied apart from it again. Unless we run from Jesus until the calluses on our hearts match the calluses on our feet, we'll be driven back again to the romance of God. Because nothing else will do. I know this firsthand. I'm a long shot from having this whole thing pinned down, but this I promise you. What I've tasted and seen is what I want more than anything in this world. Yes, I have other wants. Contrary wants. At times, sinful wants. But what their fulfillment can do for me can never bring me the ecstasy of one second's awareness that, somewhere just beyond the veil, Jesus smiles.

5. Rom. 8:6; Gal. 5:17

You Would Ask Me

In late 2001, a movie called *A Beautiful Mind* scrolled across theater marquees and, fifteen months later, waltzed its way on the stage of the 74th Academy Awards to receive an Oscar for Best Picture. The film was based on the life of John Nash, a Nobel Laureate in Economics, who endured the harrowing breadth of his entire adult lifetime with paranoid schizophrenia. Nash is played so brilliantly and exquisitely by Russell Crowe that you can feel the hot breath of his sanity gasping for air way down in your own set of lungs.

Or, maybe it was just me. Well, and others like me who have greatly loved someone with mental illness or felt, as I have, the cold kiss of madness close to their own lips, clamoring to come in and unhinge their minds. I have to make myself remember when I write a book like this that many women have not been where I've been or seen what I've seen. People really do exist out there with healthy upbringings, track records of sound decisions, and histories unstained by head-hanging shame. I know some of them. You may be one of them. I desperately want those things for my generational line. All have experienced pain, disappointment, stress, and confusion. All have sinned and, in one way or another, let themselves and at least a few others down. Everybody needs a Savior. But not all have shimmied so perilously close to the edge that they still wake up in a cold sweat from nightmares of the rock giving way. Not all have squeezed their eyes tight in the black of the night, pressing their Bibles hard to their foreheads, trying to block out the terrifying prospect that they've tumbled past the point of no return and can kiss their sanity good-bye.

The truth was, I hadn't passed it and neither have you or you wouldn't be perched there on the other side of this page. You may feel scarred by it. So do I. But it didn't kill us. Here we are, you and me. And God may have used the season to kill the destructive, fleshly side of us that would have eventually killed us. The enemy of our souls was hell-bent on convincing me that I had, in fact, gone too far to return and rebound and I'd supplied him ample evidence to build an airtight case. I was approaching my mid-thirties when my past came calling at the precise moment my present felt so unbearable that, if it were my future, I'd have been sorely tempted to bale. My history became a wild-haired false prophet in sackcloth screaming in a bullhorn until he was hoarse: *this is who you are, this is who you were, this is who you will always be.* My brush with madness would not bury me six-feet under to fertilize daisies, nor drive me off the cliff into an abyss. It would hurl me instead to the medical practice of my sole panacea. In Revelation 1:8, He calls Himself *the Alpha and the Omega . . . who is, and who was, and who is to come, the Almighty* (NIV). Exactly what you and I need to make it on this planet in one whole piece:

The One who *is*, for all that we are.

The One who *was*, for all that we were.

The One who *is to come*, for all that we will be.

He is *almighty*, the Scripture says, over all things present, all things past, and all things future. As it turned out, I did not need a dozen specialists. The stethoscope of the omnipotent physician would stretch with slack to attend to every throb of my heart from birth to death. To my tremendous astonishment, neither it nor I would snap.

My relational experience with mental illness has not been a deeper education than what occurred within the walls of my own mind, but the course has extended far longer. For reasons known to God alone, I was predestined, I believe, to deeply love a number of people whose minds teetered back and forth between bruised and broken. I have no doubt that this lifelong overlap is one reason among many that God made sure I faced with fright the fragility of my own mind. It's harder to judge. When I'm tempted to, I whisper to myself, *Girlfriend, you could be one little crisis from crazy.* That usually does it.

Life's just complicated, isn't it? Case in point, the complexities of doing life in close community with people suffering with certain mental illnesses. The question does not always apply but where it does, how much or how little of their hurtful behavior can they be held responsible for? Are they doing the best they can or are they ever occasionally using it to take advantage of you? Are you, in that moment of question, sinfully unfeeling or just completely exhausted? These matters are not always cut and dry. The angles of both sufferer and supporter are rife with complications.

We each have our own sets of variables but, if I were a betting woman, I'd bet good money that you wish things could simply be simpler. That answers could just be plainer. Dealing with hormones alone can be advanced calculus. Add stepchildren to that or, let's say, aging parents and trying to keep their medication straight. You might be sorting out the frustrating mess in your bank account from the identity theft of your debit card. Maybe you have a third grader with learning disabilities. You're so thankful he doesn't have anything life threatening but, Lord in heaven, it's getting complicated.

Take that relationship where you're trying to trust somebody who's begged you to do so, but you're suspicious that something is going on behind your back again. You know you may be making it up. You know you're not perfect either. You wish you could see black or white, but so much looks murky and gray. Or, maybe your biggest complications are not personal. They're professional. The politics at work are driving you crazy. You have no idea who is friend or foe. Every time you turn around, your company is being restructured and any shred of team-mentality has turned into cutthroat competition.

It doesn't even have to be a big situation for your soul to beg for simplicity. All it takes is updating your cell phone and losing all your contacts or trying to keep up with a jillion passwords or attempting to reach a real person on the phone at the pharmacy instead of an automated operator. Nothing is easy, not even ordering fried chicken at a drive thru on your way home from work.

The entrée only or the meal deal? Just chicken.

Regular or extra crispy? Extra crispy.

Mild or spicy? Uh, how spicy is it? *Not very.* Okay, I'll have spicy.

Do you want dipping sauce? Yes.

What kind? What kinds do you have? [Lists them.] I'll take sweet and sour.

Is that the only kind? I forgot to mention honey mustard. Want it? No thanks.

Okay, how many? [Confusion] How many what?

How many sweet and sours? Um, four I guess.

Did you want a drink with that? No, that'll be it.

You're not getting a drink? No. Thank you, though.

With all that spicy chicken? I thought it wasn't that spicy.

It's spicy enough for a soft drink. Do you want one or do you want to start over and change your chicken order to mild? No, no, no. I'll stick with spicy.

What drink would you like to go with that? [Pause] I'll have a Coke.

Diet or regular? Regular. [In case diet sounds a tad absurd with fried chicken.]

What size? Medium, I guess.

Want to upsize for 29 cents? No. Medium's good.

Cash or plastic? Plastic.

Is it debit or credit?

By the time you pull up to the first window to pay and the second window to get your chicken, they've asked more questions than an online dating application. Now you wish you'd gotten the regular instead of extra crispy because you've lost the will to chew.

Does everything on earth have to be complicated?

In the concluding scene of *A Beautiful Mind*, the camera pans an evening-lit auditorium, swiftly transporting the viewer's gaze from a multi-tiered balcony to the lowest floor and then toward the stage. The exuberant applause of the audience sounds like heavy rain on a metal roof. Every seat is taken, row upon row of prestigious men in tuxes and noble women wrapped in the best of their wardrobes. It's Stockholm in the film and the year is 1994. The occasion is the Nobel Prize ceremony. The lens of the camera falls on John Nash, the recipient, uneasy and advanced in age, as he steps to a large wooden podium edged in greenery. His speech is short and to the point, the movement of his mouth and the sound of his voice each labored enough to rid the audience of the convenience of forgetting his ordeal.

In the countless times I've seen the film, I have never once watched the scene without crying. You really need the hauntingly beautiful music to start piping in around the fourth line as it does in the film if you mean to roll off your couch in the fetal position. We don't have the luxury of the soundtrack here, but maybe the brief monologue will still be effective accompanied by nothing but flat ink. Still, I'm going to have a hard time typing it and not holding my knees and rocking. In his acceptance speech in the film, the Nobel Laureate in Economics, an inarguable genius of formulas, says these measured words:

> *I've always believed in numbers and the equations*
> *and logics that lead to reason.*
> *But after a lifetime of such pursuits, I ask,*
> *"What truly is logic?"*
> *"Who decides reason?"*
> *My quest has taken me through the physical, the metaphysical,*
> *the delusional—and back.*
> *And I have made the most important discovery of my career,*
> *the most important discovery of my life:*
> *It is only in the mysterious equations of love*
> *that any logic or reasons can be found.*
> *I'm only here tonight because of you.*[1]

The rest of the audience gets lost in the shadow of one beautiful face. It is that of a wife, equally advanced in years, who'd ridden the terrifying ride right at his side. In the hearing of the auspicious crowd, he addresses her alone with two concluding statements:

---

1. Taken from the movie *It's a Beautiful Mind*, screenplay by Akiva Goldsman.

You are the reason I am.
You are all my reasons.

I bawl like a baby through this scene over all its obvious tenderness. Nash's story as portrayed in this film becomes a profound illustration of monstrous obstacles overcome and of rare individuals who have the stamina and support to keep getting back up after the unthinkable and make their contribution to this troubled world. Those things drench me. But what nearly drowns me is the extraordinary intensity of any journey that brings a person to a place to say to another with riveting certainty, "You are all my reasons." How many reasons have washed away like words scribbled in wet sand to be able to chisel that claim in concrete? In different wording,

You are the only reason I've made it. You alone.
Here in the final winter of this brutal and beautiful
life, you are all my reasons.

Kills me.

Right here, over the crust of this earth where our lives swing like pendulums between the complicated and catastrophic, every now and again something simple comes along. *The mysterious equations of love*, Nash's character remarked. This divine love we've ruminated over for nine solid chapters is mysterious alright. It cannot help but be. Its Captain is. But the equation that adds up to a mortal life captive to this divine, mysterious love is not complicated at all.

Ask for it.

That's it.

I've expended thousands of words to finally reach these three:

Ask for it.

Has anything stirred around in you, turning these pages? Anything fast asleep started twitching? Any part of you that's bored thinking that maybe a little adventure might not be so bad? Anybody with something missing thinking it's at least worth seeing if an audacious fiery lifelong love could be the link? Every single one of us is looking for *the one*. It's the stuff of fairy tales. This one person that completely does it for us. Some of us have had dreams come true and embraced a flesh-and-blood version of *the one*. I'd be heartbroken if you misunderstood me to minimize the priceless gift of that kind of love and satisfaction. You are outrageously blessed if you could stand at a microphone and confess with stark-raving honesty before thousands,

You are the reason I am.

I have a mighty good man in Keith Moore. He is the only guy on this earth for me. We have been through seasons we shouldn't have survived. We have chosen to fall back in love again hundreds of times. We have laughed so hard our sides have split. We have danced ourselves silly in the kitchen while smothered steak simmered on the stove. But I couldn't always come through for him nor could he for me. Other times we could have, but we refused to. We'd know what the other really needed from us and, so, instead of giving it, we'd withhold it. It was power. We don't do that kind of thing much anymore but we are still creatures with innate partialities to our own selves. Often enough one of us will want to go out to a movie (Keith, believe it or not) and the other will beg to rent one on iTunes and watch it at home. One of us will be in a talkative mood and the other will be thorny. We get defensive sometimes when one of us overspends and we get grumpy every time tax season rolls around. One of us is known to leave chips and bean dip open on the coffee table in the den all night for the other one to pick up in the morning when she gets up. But I won't say whom. And it's normal.

But you and I haven't stirred up all this dust for something normal. We can do normal by ourselves. We're talking about a love that is extraordinary, remember? Supremely supernatural. We're talking about being swept up with *the One* you can't tire out and you can't run off. *The One* who still calls you Beautiful at your ugliest and pulls you up at your lowest. *The One* who doesn't have to struggle to forgive you. *The One* who really does keep no record of wrongs. *The One* who doesn't have to go to counseling to stay with you. We're talking about coming alive to an honest-to-God acceptance that we are audaciously loved and drumming up the audacity to boldly love Him back. *That*, I believe to my bones, would be the most important discovery of our lives. The craziest part is that it's not hard to get.

Ask for it.

Do you remember early on in chapter 2 when I brought up the story in John 4 about Jesus and the Samaritan woman? We locked in on one powerful phrase Jesus spoke to the unsuspecting woman who'd been on a mad spree to fill her emptiness:

"If you only knew."

In case you've done a fair amount of living since that chapter, no worries at all. It just so happens I still have the segment handy. Take another look at it.

> *Jacob's well was there; and Jesus, tired from the long walk, sat wearily beside the well about noontime. Soon a Samaritan woman came to draw water, and Jesus said to her, "Please give me a drink." He was alone at the time because his disciples had gone into the village to buy some food. The woman was surprised, for Jews refuse to have anything to do with Samaritans. She said to Jesus, "You are a Jew, and I am a Samaritan woman. Why are you asking me for a drink?" Jesus replied, "If you only knew the gift God has for you and who you are speaking to, you would ask me, and I would give you living water." (John 4:6–10 NLT)*

Did you catch the four words that complement the phrase, "If you only knew"?

"You would ask Me."

Weigh those four words until they sink down somewhere deep. To some of us, the spiritual concept could be brand new. To others, it's so familiar that you're already tempted to glaze over like a donut fresh out of the grease. If that's you, throw back a shot of espresso with that donut, stay awake here, and stick those four-word phrases together:

"If you only knew . . . you would ask Me."

Those two phrases would apply to anything Jesus makes wholeheartedly available and urges us in Scripture to receive. To us, in the context of this book, they can mean something like this:

If you only knew the gift I could give you and the ecstatic satisfaction of My Spirit within you . . .

If you only knew what this relationship could be like and how boldly I love you and continually pursue you . . .

If you only know how fully I could bring you to life and gift you and use you and bring to redemption everything you've endured . . .

If you only knew the life you were born to live and how worth your trouble it would be . . .

If you only knew the transformative power of divine love received and reciprocated . . .

If you only knew how courageous you would be if you were caught up with Me . . .

Then You would ask Me.

All of our asking could still be a waste of breath and dust in the wind without the four glorious words that follow in John 4:10.

I would give you.

Those three groups of four words in that single statement of Jesus form an equation with a mass-energy relationship that puts Einstein's $E = mc^2$ to shame.

If you only knew + you would ask Me = I would give you

The equation is so simple that, somewhere down in our belief systems, we don't even see how it could work. It can seem one step up from believing that Santa Claus can manage to get his big belly down our chimneys without getting caught by his beard in a bird nest and then he's going to leave us the exact presents we requested in the letters we mailed to the North Pole. If we've been in the faith for a while, we might firmly believe that Jesus saves and that we're going to heaven when we die, but we're apt to leave the whole *just-ask* thing for new believers who need the extra incentives. Maybe we think we've learned the hard way that *just-ask* doesn't work. We've somehow matured our way out of expecting anything other than life after death. But here's the thing: the equation *does* work. It is guaranteed to work. No matter what anybody has ever told us or what we've told ourselves based on our own calculations, this is word-for-word what Scripture says:

> *Now this is the confidence we have before Him: Whenever we ask anything according to His will, He hears us. And if we know that He hears whatever we ask, we know that we have what we have asked Him for.* (1 John 5:14–15)

I know what I'd say right now if you and I could switch places and I were in an argumentative mood. "But, see? There's a catch! To get what you ask for, you have to ask *according to His will* and who on God's green earth knows what that is?"

Good question. Sometimes we honestly don't know what God's will is. We'll think we do. We'll pray like we do—then our hopes won't come true. This, however, doesn't happen to be one of those times when God's will is mysterious. Take a fresh look at Mark 12:28–30.

> *One of the scribes approached. When he heard them debating and saw that Jesus answered them well, he asked Him, "Which command is the most important of all?" "This is the most important," Jesus answered: Listen, Israel! The Lord our God, the Lord is One. Love the Lord your God with all your heart, with all your soul, with all your mind, and with all your strength.*

God, whose sovereignty will exceed the expanse of the universe, wants nothing more for you or for me than for us to love Him with every atom in us. Nothing is more adamantly and inarguably God's will for our lives. This is uncontested priority to Him. Everything else comes second at best.

The axis of our approach shifts dramatically when we know beyond a doubt that we're perfectly aligned, asking God for something He is more anxious to give than we are to receive.

> *Now this is the confidence we have before Him* . . . (1 John 5:14)

Confidence in prayer changes everything: the tone of our voice, our words of choice, our posture, our passion, our presence of joy. We turn our faces heavenward as true believers in what we're asking, not just apologetic beggars panhandling a cautious God with tight pockets. We approach Him full of unshakable faith that we are going to get the audacious love we request because it is God's supreme desire for man. *And woman.* We take this request to His throne with no backup plan if He doesn't come through. No bracing ourselves for disappointment. We get to ask for it with flamboyant expectation because our receiving it is as sure as our requesting it. This gift of confidence means that, with the first breath, we get to ask Him—and, with the second breath, we get to thank Him. Start it from the very beginning. Be outrageous in your thanksgiving. You can even break out in a little tap dance over it if that's your kind of thing. Or, if you're a runner, go run wildly in the wind with incarnate gratitude. For the love of God, do something. Show Him some enthusiasm. He'll love it.

Because here's the thing: not one of you, regardless of your background, living conditions, relationships, or religion, will be turned down. Every one of you who earnestly asks God to grant you a bold and daring answering-love for Jesus, marked by originality and verve, are going to receive it. It's as good as done. And you keep asking for the rest of your days. Notice the verb tenses expressed to perfection in the *Holman Christian Standard Bible.*

"Keep asking, and it will be given to you. Keep searching, and you will find. Keep knocking, and the door will be opened to you. For everyone who asks receives, and the one who searches finds, and to the one who knocks, the door will be opened." (Matt. 7:7–8)

I'm positive the equation works because God promises us in His Word that it does. I also know the equation works from personal experience. In my late twenties, I sat slack-jawed at the sight of someone who loved Him and loved His Word in a way I'd not witnessed in a lifetime of attending church. A former football player, he was tall and imposing and almost as thick as he was wide. Nothing but solid muscle. And, at times, when he taught, his voice would break and tears would well in his eyes for nothing but love of the Savior and the Scriptures. I was flabbergasted. I ran to my car after class, slammed the door, burst into tears, and exclaimed to God, "I don't know what that was but I want it!" God's response to me did not come audibly, of course, or in an exact succession of words but it thundered in my soul in a way I have no trouble translating.

Ask Me for it. Pray for it. Seek it with everything in you. And for the rest of your days.

I began that very day, that very moment, unsure of exactly how to define the bold love for Jesus I'd seen in that man or what it might look like on me. I asked for it again this morning. The most repetitive request I've raised to Jesus for three solid decades has been this: *give me a heart to love You more than anything I can see or touch. Grant me love for You, Jesus. This is what I want more than anything. Be the driving desire of my life.* If we've ever run into one another in an airport or a Starbucks or at church or in Bible study and you've asked me what you could pray for me, I have over and over said this one thing above all others: *pray for me to love Jesus and make it across that finish line more taken with Him than anything on this earth.*

I write these words with tears stinging in my eyes: I have done woefully foolish things in my life and made an unhappy host of pathetic decisions. Most of my advancement on the spiritual pavement has come by falling, tripping, or stumbling forward. Despite all my failures and frailties, God, in His unfathomable grace, has granted me and keeps granting the chief request He planted in my heart all those years ago. This one thing—this love, this singular driving desire—originated, fueled, and consumed by the Holy Spirit—has fed any spiritual discipline, every second of serving, and any remotest hint of obedience to God's will that I've ever mustered. I'd been trying to be a good girl in my earlier twenties. Trying to perform to make God happy. That evening, when I slammed the car door and cried out to God to give me whatever that man possessed, something glorious broke loose. God let Passion out of the gate like a racehorse on Red Bull and that thing stampeded over the hindquarters of Performance like it was an old mule in its great-great-grandma's shoes. I'd still have harsh seasons ahead as we always do, but never again, would obligation drive my devotion. I'd tasted something I'd no longer be able to live long without.

When Jesus answered the scribe's question concerning the most important commandment of all, He supplied every willing reader with the one key that He well knew would unlock every other treasure. It is the way God ordained it. Love alone would have the power to make life work. When my life is excruciating, this one thing makes it still worth living: I have been caught up in a sacred love affair for thirty years that I've never gotten over. This is what I want for my children. This is what I want for my grandchildren. I can be certain they'll follow Jesus if their hearts can't help it.

In the last few chapters, we've hammered the point that, except in matters of survival, *want* is a far more powerful motivator than *need*. You can take this one to the bank: we humans desire most what we love most. It's as simple as that. If you come to audaciously love Jesus, you will audaciously seek Jesus. You will audaciously serve Jesus. You will audaciously show Jesus to people who don't know Him. You will audaciously surf angry seas to fulfill your holy calling. You won't be able to help yourself. You will want to be alive and awake to His company because you automatically want who you love. Listen, I'm not trying to put words in your mouth. You get the privilege of freestyling with any way you want to say it and any way you want to pray it but, for those of you who could use a kick-start, I'll throw out a seven-word prayer you can start saying to Jesus this second that will turn your beautiful, breathtaking self completely inside out:

Be the driving desire of my life.

There you will find *the One*. And, one of these days, when your days are almost done, and you've thanked every wonderful human being for all they've meant to you, you will, then, be able to lock your eyes toward *the One* alone and say to Him with a riveting certainty that takes the whole house down,

You are the reason I am.
You are all my reasons.

A Love for All Loves

When you move out of a house you've lived in for twenty-seven years, you're liable to relive all twenty-seven of them, even the ones you'd rather not. You don't relive the years in order, of course. You relive them in desultory piles you pull from that shadowy chamber where lightbulbs never work and angels fear to tread: the attic. It is domicile purgatory: the holding place where people like me hurl heavy-duty trash bags full of things we want out of the way but can't throw away. You don't label the bags either or you might actually know what is in them twenty-plus years later when you move. Instead, you are forced to go through every one of them lest you throw away the hairpiece your great-aunt left you—then, right there among your kids' old Cabbage Patch dolls and stuffed animals, you discover the added bonus of a mouse skeleton.

I'd sworn and declared to Keith Moore that he'd never budge me from our home of so many years. We'd raised our children there. They'd gone from strollers to big wheels to bikes and to cars in that driveway. I'd watched them play basketball in that driveway from the kitchen window while I loaded the dishwasher. I'd spied on each of our daughters through the mini-blinds in the den when they got home from dates so that I could check on whether or not they and their boyfriends were kissing. If they tarried in the car uncomfortably long and I perceived considerable lip contact, Keith and I on occasion raised the mini-blinds, stood right in front of the window and kissed theatrically. That usually broke it up.

In that backyard we'd buried dogs we'd had so long, their furry dark faces had turned snow white and loved like there was no tomorrow. No way was I leaving those graves. We'd had the same great neighbors for ages who were slightly terrified by the line of work I was in, but had grown to love us nonetheless and let their kids play with ours. Once, when a guy from animal control tried to impound one of our dogs that had escaped the backyard, my neighbor told him that the owner was in religious work and that, if he dared take that dog, an awful curse would fall upon him. I need not have to tell you that he let the dog go with impressive haste. These were neighbors you can't replace. They never said a word about Keith duct taping real deer horns to the festive white-wire reindeer we put in the front yard every Christmas.

I told all of this to Keith every time he brought up wishing we could move. I'd start with the sentimental things and, when he appeared unmoved, I hit him where it hurt: *You'll have to clean out the attic.* I told him no few times that the only way we'd be able to deal with that attic was to set a match to it and that I wasn't even sure bodies of air conditioning repairmen from the eighties wouldn't be discovered up there dried into jerky. *Do you really want to take that chance?* I demanded to know.

Indeed he did.

He arranged for an industrial trash-disposal company to drop off a gargantuan army-green pod in our driveway and come back for it a week later. I knew then we'd have to move. I was just as glad that I couldn't see the neighbors for the pod. But, every twenty trash bags or so, something turned up worth shrieking over all the scattering roaches. I sat on the floor of my den one day with a mound of pages six inches high and several feet wide, dated as far back as the births of my children. They were talks I'd given as a young speaker. Every page was run amok with exclamation points and every message—bar none—concluded with a selection of poetry. Would that I could say that each special piece had not been composed by my own hand. I'd written a myriad of poems for all possible occasions including the Fourth of July. The one that appeared with the greatest frequency was a compelling piece in which I'd incorporated the names of every soap opera on daytime television. What Christian speaker worth her salt could not put a title like *One Life to Live* to use? In an ideal world, someone would have loved me enough to whisper three magic words in my ear: *Helen Steiner Rice*. Alas, this is no ideal world and, if you need further proof, I have a few poems you can read.

I found a small stack of mimeographed pages in the pile that I'd run off for churches that contacted me as a potential speaker for their women's gatherings. Each identical sheet was a repertoire of twelve titles of messages I had to offer and their brief descriptions. I'd typed this up myself as a one-page ready response to the inevitable inquiry: *What do you speak on?* It didn't take long for me to catch on to the fact that the more topics one had, the better one's chances would be, so I sought to broaden my range. Hence, the twelve.

Most of the inquiries in those days were for luncheons or dinners which took place in fellowship halls and included a fashion show of ladies' apparel showcasing such unquestionable modesty that the selections were nothing at all if not cumbersome. The speaker was invited to bring a word of inspiration that she would deliver toward the end of the event as the women ate their dessert. If you're the visual sort, perhaps you'll relish knowing that it was usually cherry crisp on a white paper plate, crowned with a scoop of nondairy topping that held the perfect shape of the serving spoon for hours on end.

Since I was still teaching aerobics classes at my church gym, what better title among the twelve could showcase a message on Christian fitness than *Fit for a King*? Some things are no-brainers. Lest anyone think leg warmers conveyed a lack of depth, the very next title was *The Sold Out Servant*. I feel certain this message suggested that, if you didn't teach vacation Bible school or at least play in the handbell choir at your church, you were running a high risk of going to—well—a place far, far south of heaven with a high, high heat index. This edifying seminar clearly preceded the holy beating that would befriend me with grace.

None of the other titles in my repertoire raised my eyebrows like this riveting caption: *The Many Hats of God*. The description promised a moving message on the many roles God plays in the life of a Christian. Though I have repressed the memory in order to survive a history of chronic corniness, I feel quite sure I took along hats. All for Jesus. Several days later at our neighborhood Mexican restaurant, I had to force myself to look away from the huge sombrero hanging on the wall over our booth. For a solid week, I couldn't shake the image of Jesus wearing it.

Sorting twenty-seven years of trash in search of treasures, I found a shiny red shirt box, taped shut, with the words *Beth's Keepsakes* written in black marker in the penmanship of my young adulthood. Inside I found things like the teacher's certificate I'd received from the State of Texas after graduating from college and meeting the requirements for teaching high school political science and English. I discovered a class picture from first grade and undeniable evidence that I'd long-since had hair of substantial size. I also found a card from Keith. I'd collect stacks of them through the years but this one alone appeared in the shiny red box and for an understandably good reason. It was the first card Keith ever gave me and I had not laid eyes on it for decades. He'd presented it to me not long after we started dating in the Fall term of our junior year of college.

You know how it is. If you have the remotest hint that a relationship is going anywhere, you guard the first correspondence with your life. If it's a text, you take a screen shot. Of course, if the person turns out to be a jerk, you trash it after you wave it around in a fury, leverage it, and talk about it obsessively. But, if the relationship endures, you'll glance back at it and nod, recognizing in the clarity of hindsight that, hidden somewhere in that initial exchange, was a hint about where it would go.

The style of that first card from Keith was vintage late seventies with light purple tones in a shiny cellophane card sleeve. A young couple is standing on the beach in one another's arms, both wearing bell-bottom jeans. The sea in the background is glassy-smooth and untroubled, their powerful love rendering all well with the world. A gentle breeze has tousled the couples' hair but just enough to rule out a good, solid shellacking with a blue can of Aqua Net. The sun is setting on the horizon behind them as if it rose that very morning for them alone. It is a simple player in their larger story. A vivid beam from that ball of fire is spraying sheaths of light just beneath the couple's lips, making a silhouette of their timeless kiss. Only two words appear on the card, written in romantic white cursive against the pale purple sky hovering above the lovers:

I'M SORRY . . .

Perfect. I rolled onto my stomach and beat the floor, laughing. I have no idea what Keith had done but I'm pretty sure it wasn't the last time. No two words in the entire English language could have more aptly captioned a picture of the relationship that would unfold over the days, weeks, months, seasons, years, and decades to come. Thank God for those two words. We have each worn them into nubs.

The pairing up of our copious problems gave birth to our horde of apologies. Had being molested not been sufficient to tip my relationships out of kilter, I'd also grown up in an atmosphere of pronounced instability. I've come to believe that the effects of the long-term instability rivaled those of the shorter-term abuse. I wore fear like bones wear skin. Keith, on the other hand, had trauma, tragedy, and devastating loss looming over his shoulders like monstrous giants. He'd miraculously survived a house fire that stole his older brother's life. They were both under five years old, playing together in the garage when a gas can tipped close to a water heater. The flames left scars on Keith's soul that vastly exceeded those on his legs. Their home was engulfed in a thick smoke of sadness that continued to choke them long after the fire was put out. They reached out for support and worked hard to get back on their feet then, unfathomably, his younger sister died of an aneurysm when we were in our early twenties. It nearly killed all of us.

Keith and I did not have what it took to make it. We'd each been through too much and needed too much. Other close relationships in my life shouldn't have endured with any measure of health or pleasure either. But many of them did. Keith has his own story of how he made it and what God used to prosper his penniless soul but I've been telling you mine through every page you've turned in this book. Chasing after Jesus Christ on the bare feet of audacious love has panted life into every other decent relationship I have. It has not stolen from them. It has spared them. He alone keeps me from making gods of mortals. He alone supplies what I'd have tried and failed to get from countless others.

If I'd been sitting on the other side of this book and this concept had been new to me, my first fear would have been how a fiery relationship with Jesus would affect my other relationships. What, after all, does a relationship with God that becomes more real to you than anything you can see or touch do to those within your physical reach? Wouldn't basic mathematics tell you that putting everything in one place subtracts it from all others?

Who hasn't watched a really good friend fall head over heels in love and drop off the face of the earth? Nothing else meant anything to her, including you, it seemed. All other relationships were sacrificed like common pigeons on the blazing altar of the new bond. Even if the romance burned so hot that it soon burnt out, the friendships put on hold aren't quite the same. We've all resented loves that replaced or displaced us.

But divine affection is altogether different. It does not subtract from other loves. It supplies them. It does not detract from them. It gives them their proper dignity and their rightful place. When God called us to love Him with everything in us, He knew we could not do it without Him. He knew that He Himself would have to provide the affection to ever consistently see it returned. For this reason *this hope will not disappoint us, because God's love has been poured out in our hearts through the Holy Spirit who was given to us* (Rom. 5:5). When God issued the command for the highest love of human hearts to be directed solely to Him, it wasn't to hoard it all for Himself. He meant to sanctify it and multiply it. Our affection for Him leaps straight up like a fountain to be filtered by His fingers then spilled clean on those around us.

You've seen this segment numerous times over the course of these eleven chapters but take one last glance with the additional commandment that builds our point:

28One of the scribes approached. When he heard them debating and saw that Jesus answered them well, he asked Him, "Which command is the most important of all?"

29"This is the most important," Jesus answered:

Listen, Israel! The Lord our God, the Lord is One. 30Love the Lord your God with all your heart, with all your soul, with all your mind, and with all your strength.

31"The second is: Love your neighbor as yourself. There is no other command greater than these." (Mark 12:28–31)

The tendency of our human nature—at its best—is to reverse the order and make the second command first and the first command second. In other words, first love the ones you can see, then love the One you can't. It seems perfectly reasonable but, in the exchange of places, we choke the supply and toss the filter. The irony is that the second most important command cannot displace the first without robbing itself. To love God more is never to love people less. It's to love people best. It's to relieve them of the responsibility of being your false Christ. It's to keep their sins against you from being unforgivable and your sins against them from being ignorable. It's to guard them from our mean-streaks and strong human tendencies to respond to disappointment with punishment. It's to keep the people close by from cutting their wrists on the razor-sharp blades of our insecurities. It's to dull the edge of our cravings to be adored. It's to untie the double knots of codependency. It's to let the affirmations of others be the overflow and not the essential source of our emotional survival. To love God is to guard man.

Divine affection is a floorless wellspring with the capacity to water every inch of ground your life will ever cover. It makes you capable of loving someone you can't and appreciating someone you don't—and not because God suddenly gives you a case of cataracts to keep you from seeing what drives you crazy. God's love is not blind. Divine love outsourced to human hearts is smart, knowing, and discerning.[1] It is not capped but it is also not easily conned. True love sees. You set your sight with laser-thin focus on Christ alone and, suddenly, your peripheral vision tears wide open and, there, staring straight ahead, you catch a glimpse of an entire vista.

> *For with You is life's fountain.*
> *In Your light we will see light.* (Ps. 36:9)

The catch is, you plant your feet on a land of these wonders only on the other side of faith. We are called by Jesus to jeopardize everything we have and everything we are on this one supreme love, counting all else as loss for *the surpassing value of knowing Christ.*[2] Only after the risk do we discover the reward: with Him came everything else of ultimate value. Jesus gave voice to a promise in Matthew 6:33 that we can press against our pounding hearts when we fear what we could lose:

> *But seek first the kingdom of God and His righteousness,*
> *and all these things will be provided for you.*

To clip the concept in this chapter into its simplest terms, to audaciously love Jesus Christ is not only the best thing you could ever do for yourself. It's the best thing you could do for those around you even if, at first, they beg to differ. Every relationship in your life stands to benefit from your bold, adventurous affection for Jesus Christ, not because you

---

1. Phil. 1:9–10
2. Phil. 3:7–8; Matt. 10:37–39

will run them down with a gospel eighteen-wheeler, but because you will walk the gospel out right in front of them. Audacious is not obnoxious. If our spiritual fire burns people instead of warming them, we have zeal without knowledge.[3] When time affords us the luxury—and it doesn't always—the most effective gospel is show and tell. You share Jesus with your heart by the way you love, with your hands by the things you do, and, yes, of course, you share Jesus with your mouth. Sooner or later, you won't be able to keep from it. Audacious love unties the shiest tongue.

It also makes people curious about you. We hardly know what to do with individuals who are secure enough not to grapple in one way or another for our adoration, affirmation, or attention. In a world system belching with bondage, all it takes to be an anomaly is a little bit of liberty. In a media stream of terrible news, all it takes to stick out is a little bit of hope. In a cultural climate increasing in cold-heartedness, all it takes to be noticed is a little bit of warmth. In a sea of people making constant demands, all it takes to float to the top is to let somebody off the hook. On a loud social stage of tap-dancing narcissists, a time comes when those in the orchestra who don't blow their own horns do tend to finally get heard. Mark my word, people will get curious. That's why 1 Peter 3:15–16 says,

> [15]*Always be prepared to give an answer to everyone who asks you to give the reason for the hope that you have. But do this with gentleness and respect,*
>
> > [16]*keeping a clear conscience, so that those who speak maliciously against your good behavior in Christ may be ashamed of their slander.* (NIV)

---

3. Prov. 19:2 and Rom. 10:2

Audaciously loving Jesus doesn't preclude needing people. God fashioned us for fellowship. We need human contact. We need human touch. We'll still need friendships and siblings and social outlets. We'll still want to be liked and want to be loved and we still wish for romance. But indescribable freedom comes when we no longer need humans to save us. We set people free to love us in a way they never otherwise could have when we no longer hold them responsible for giving us the lives we were born to live. Our friends can't do that for us. Our husbands can't do that for us. Our children can't do that for us. Our employers can't do that for us. Our banks can't do that for us. Our schools can't do that for us. Our churches can't do that for us. The very best of counselors can't do that for us and God knows I believe in counselors.

Only Jesus can do that for us. Only He knows the end from the beginning. Only He knows why He seeded us in this soil at this season in history and what He purposed to accomplish and grow through us. But this you can count on: it's something good. It's something that means something. It's something you would not want to miss for the entire world. It's the reason why you're here.

This brings me to the twitchy point where I need to write some words that may sound cold but, if I close this book without saying them, I will have launched the message with boldness and ended it with cowardice. So, this is it. Any relationship that ultimately and absolutely cannot withstand your audacious love for Jesus will almost certainly be a snare to you. If you remain strongly influenced by it, it will trip you up over and over, fog your spiritual vision, cloud your mind with confusion, and keep you in a perpetual state of frustration. Any profoundly controlling relationship that curtails your right to love Jesus Christ with your whole heart, soul, mind, and strength could cost you your calling. It could suck the air out of the lungs of the life you were born to live.

If your closest friends are opposed to your audacious pursuit of Jesus, add some new ones who share it. If you're willing to look beyond your usual circle but still can't find them, ask God to round them up and bring them your way. Keep your eyes wide open. Resist the thought that they need to look or act a certain way or be a specific age or color. This isn't high school. Well, unless it is. If you're a high school student and you've stuck with this book all this time, you've just won my heart forever. Please find a way to let me know. Regardless of your age, ask Jesus to bring people along who stir you up to love Him, chase after Him, and bask in Him in a way you wouldn't have without them. You may have a spiritual mother or daughter out there somewhere just waiting for you. Someone who will end up becoming dearer to you than your own skin. We need fellow sojourners in our walk of faith in the worst way. We need not only to worship beside them, but pray with them, and seek Jesus with them. We need to laugh hard with them and be ridiculous with them. There is no estimating the revival we could have in America if we were all less convinced that being unlikeable is a Christian virtue.

I'm about to get a little bolder here but I'll be quick about it. Anyway, if this book isn't about boldness, it has no viable point. I extend the following counsel to you with tremendous compassion based on what I've learned from Scripture and seen over and over *and over again* in thirty years of working with women: If you are serious about or engaged to someone who can't tolerate your audacious, adventurous love for Jesus, do not marry him. If you're already married to him, for the love of God, don't pack up and leave him, but do start praying wildly for Jesus to steal his heart, not just for your sake but for his.

This book is written from one woman to another but every biblical concept within it is equally true for men. At the end of a life well-lived, Jesus is the sum total of all their reasons, too. Pray that the man in your life, if this applies, will come to know it if he doesn't. In the meantime, guard him from feeling like he has to compete with God or he will resent Him. First Peter 3:1–2 tells us to win an unbelieving husband over by the way we live. Let your words be few and your heart be huge. Keep praying that God will make him willing to be won. If he's not, be forthright in prayer, spilling before God—completely unfiltered—how you feel and what you'd hoped and where you hurt. Guard yourself against resentment, too. Call Jesus boldly to your aid and your defense. Ask Him to give you profuse wisdom and precise direction and other outlets for expressing your faith. Ask Him to blaze a trail right before your eyes where you can plant your feet toward every purpose you were born for. Have the insistent audacity to ask God to grant your man favor toward your faith so that, should he never choose to share it, he will still bless you to flourish in it.

Keith became a Christian right before we got engaged (how's that for a method of evangelism?) but he did not share my (over-) enthusiasm for Sunday school, church choir, church camp, church potluck supper, church prayer meeting, or cheesy church poetry. Clearly, he'd never played a handbell in his life nor taught vacation Bible school a single summer. I have no idea how the man endured the rampant zeal. Church had been my harbor in the storm growing up. My sanity. I loved it. I still love it. I still believe in it.

I recall with a grin first telling Keith that I was going to "work for God" and asking him if he could handle it. We had dated for several months and I had a strong suspicion we were heading toward a proposal. Understandably, he looked a bit puzzled. He paused for a moment, calculating the risk that he might not have a second chance to react well.

"What kind of work are you going to do for God?"

I responded with sincerity, feeling ridiculously silly, "I have no earthly idea."

Neither of us will ever forget the solid-gold words that tumbled out of his mouth next.

"Are you planning to be a nun?" His family heritage was Catholicism and, for the life of him, he couldn't think of any other way a woman could work for God.

"Uh, no." I mumbled. I mean, we'd just made out for the better part of an hour so I was a tad thrown.

"Okay, then," he responded with a fair measure of relief. "I can take it."

And he has taken it alright, God bless him, and, all the while, never caring one iota to be a pastor, deacon, elder, usher or anything else at church. He doesn't often read his Bible but he does on occasion love to flip through a good hymnal. Despite innumerable debates early on, Keith wants to make his spiritual contribution primarily by being a good husband to a woman in full-time ministry. It is a role he fills with tremendous strength and testosterone. He has my respect and he knows it. That's what matters to him. He could not care less who doesn't understand. That's just Keith. He's not looking to win friends and influence people. He prays for me and keeps me honest. If a man bullies me on social media, he tells me to just say when and he'll kick his tail, though in slightly more colorful terms. He kisses me a guiltless good-bye when I leave town to speak and picks me up off the floor when I get home. When he sits next to me in church, I'm glad. When he doesn't, I'm no longer mad. This is Mr. and Mrs. Keith Moore, in all our flaws and frailties, and we're making it with no few joys. We have Jesus alone to thank for that.

If you decide to really do this thing, Jesus *is* going to work it all out, even and especially when you are fresh out of ideas for bossing Him how. You watch. He will be outrageously faithful to you. If you'll be obedient to God—I mean truly obedient and not obnoxious, overbearing, and intolerable—the consequences of your obedience will be His problem, not yours. Hand Him over the fallout that comes from following Him. He loves every person in your life infinitely more than you do. He sent His Son for them, too. He understands the complications. He's reading every mind and searching every heart. He knows what it will take. Bow down and don't play God. Let Him do His job. Sometimes verve is having the nerve not to be controlling.

Remember that shiny red shirt box I found sorting through the mice skeletons? A letter my beloved grandmother had penned to me in her distinctive scrawl was tucked in that box. I was a young teenager when she wrote it to me, just two years shy of the day we'd bury her. I stared at the way she curled the letters of my name and remembered how warm she felt when I slept next to her on her feather bed as a young child. Me, a feather-light little girl next to her, a delightfully-plump lady of ample years and tears. I'd try to hang on to my side of the bed when she climbed in on hers and sunk the bed a solid twelve inches, but eventually I'd get sleepy, let go, and roll into the cleft of the rock. If I didn't smother to death before morning, I knew I'd wake up feeling, for a few glorious moments, wholehearted and secure. Holding that letter, my chest ached with longing to see her face again and hear the cadence of her voice. And I will someday.

Childhood traumas do a terrible disservice to the memory. They scribble helter-skelter over moments of simplicity, innocence, warmth, and beauty. I was loved as a girl by some wonderful people. Good things happened to me back there in that confusing amalgamation we call *growing up*. Good things happened to you, too, along the way or you wouldn't be on the other side of this page. Maybe your growing up years were nearly idyllic but more recent ones have been scraped off the screen of a bad TV movie. Or maybe none of it has been particularly awful but it simply lacked wonder. You just don't know where you fit and why you'd matter or what contribution you'd have to make. You feel neither pain nor passion nor any soul-deep sense of purpose.

Let your memory rewind to how Christ has pursued you and met you and stopped you and cornered you and pushed you and carried you— all because He found you fascinating enough to make sure you wouldn't miss Him. This dusty orb suspended in the universe just between heaven and hell bears in its air the flecks of them both. And we breathe them every day. I do not doubt that you have tasted hell on the tip of your tongue but you have also tasted heaven. Somewhere in the madness, you've suspected you were loved. Somewhere in the forsakenness, someone has been fighting for you all along.

Being mishandled by some can loom so large that we feel mishandled by all. Victimization, devastation, loss, rejection, betrayal. These kinds of things can coat the eyes with such a layer of gray that we miss the ray of light beneath our chins from the sun on the horizon. Through a smoky, distorted lens, no amount of good can offset the bad. We see in part, true enough—and the part we see is wholly bleak. Our hearts contract to protect themselves and their cramped circumference sees to it that love can't worm its way in. Our souls, on the other hand, have been ripped so wide open that nothing anyone can do will ever be enough. We clinch our eyes tightly and refuse to see when the winds and waves are stilled and a Savior walks our way right on top of the water.

But we don't have to stay that way—wounded, regretful, unseeing, and unchanging. We are not stuck. We are not lost causes at lasting relationships. The worst regret is gloriously redeemed when it ushers us on its broken arm down the aisle to a Groom we will never regret. Jesus chose you before the world spun into being at the sound of His thunderous voice. He knew everything about you when you were woven in your mother's womb. I think, just maybe, if He could leave you a card today in a shiny cellophane sleeve, it might bear a picture from the shore where He called His first followers, with a big ball of sunshine rising on the horizon. Only this time the follower He wants is you. And maybe the front of the card would say something like this:

I,
the Holy Son of God
with spectacular taste and perfect timing,
called you
and . . .

I'm not sorry.

The Best Part

We've reached the final chapter, you and I. I made you a promise from the start that I'd keep this book short hoping to high heaven that, by the time you were getting antsy to read something else, we'd have waved farewell. I don't know how many others will make it this far but you and I did. And you're the one I wrote the book for anyway.

I saved my favorite part for last. That might explain the whopping length of this wrap-up chapter. I've never been great at good byes. Before you over-anticipate and find yourself disappointed, let me clarify that I'm not saying this chapter will be the most meaningful part of the concept to every reader or the part that speaks the clearest or offers our feet the firmest concrete. But it's still my personal favorite. It is the miracle in this whole adventure with Jesus that takes me to the wedding feast in Cana and turns my water into wine.[1] This is where the band plays for me. This is where my toes start twitching and my feet are set to dancing.

The link to audacious love that we're looking to uncover in this concluding chapter is tucked into John 14:15–26. A little background will

---

1. John 2:1–12

shine the best light on the scene so work with me here for a couple of paragraphs. The cross is right around the corner. Jesus warned the disciples much earlier that He'd be arrested and killed and that He'd also be raised.[2] Here, only hours away from fulfillment, His followers were further than ever from wrapping their minds around His troubling words. Is it any wonder? A few days earlier they'd accompanied Jesus—their master, teacher, miracle-worker—into Jerusalem for the feast of Passover as He rode on the back of a colt to the cheers of a triumphant throng waving palm branches, shouting hosannas, and proclaiming Christ king.[3] Just prior to that royal welcome, He'd raised His good friend, Lazarus, from the dead after the man had been in the tomb four days. Few things in Scripture give me a broader grin than the King James rendering of this slice of the scene.

Jesus said, Take ye away the stone. Martha, the sister of him that was dead, saith unto him, Lord, by this time he stinketh: for he hath been dead four days. (John 11:39 KJV)

If this scene had happened today, someone would have caught Christ's expression on video with her cell phone. As it is, we can only imagine the face He made. But aren't we just like Martha sometimes, thinking that it's one thing to raise the dead, but another thing entirely to conquer that smell? It's a wonder Martha hadn't asked Him to hold up a second while she darted back to the house to grab a can of Lysol. Do you think, every now and then, Jesus ever wanted to gaze upward and say, *Our Father which art in Heaven, are You sure we couldn't have done*

2. Matt. 16:21
3. John 12:12–15

better than these folks? Instead, He responded to Mary with patience and long-suffering:

Said I not unto thee, that, if thou wouldest believe, thou shouldest see the glory of God? (John 11:40 KJV)

Here's my interpretation of His response and, in my imagination, He takes His own good time with it, punctuating every word with a perfect expression of absurdity: *Martha, did I not explicitly say to you that if you would believe, you would see the glory of God? And let Me assure you, Martha of Bethany, the glory of God does not stinketh.* Sure enough, out Lazarus walks, grave linens dangling, and not one person in the scene goes on record holding her nose, fanning her face, or yelping *pee-yew.*

That's sufficient background to catch us up so that we can search for the link to audacious love in John 14. Press your ear to this page and you'll hear Jesus trying to prepare His first followers for their loss, their ultimate gain, and for a reciprocal love that would identify itself through obedience:

"If you love Me, you will keep My commands. And I will ask the Father, and He will give you another Counselor to be with you forever. He is the Spirit of truth. The world is unable to receive Him because it doesn't see Him or know Him. But you do know Him, because He remains with you and will be in you. I will not leave you as orphans; I am coming to you.

"In a little while the world will see Me no longer, but you will see Me. Because I live, you will live too. In that day you will know that I am in My Father, you are in Me, and I am in you. The one

who has My commands and keeps them is the one who loves Me. And the one who loves Me will be loved by My Father. I also will love him and will reveal Myself to him."

Judas (not Iscariot) said to Him, "Lord, how is it You're going to reveal Yourself to us and not to the world?"

Jesus answered, "If anyone loves Me, he will keep My word. My Father will love him, and We will come to him and make Our home with him. The one who doesn't love Me will not keep My words. The word that you hear is not Mine but is from the Father who sent Me.

"I have spoken these things to you while I remain with you. But the Counselor, the Holy Spirit —the Father will send Him in My name—will teach you all things and remind you of everything I have told you." (vv. 15–26)

Land with both your feet on the verse right in the center: *The one who has My commands and keeps them is the one who loves Me. And the one who loves Me will be loved by My Father. I also will love him and will reveal Myself to him* (v. 21).

The reciprocal love Christ described did not diminish or contradict God's love for all humanity in any way. In the very same Gospel, we are not only told that God loves the entire unbelieving world but, in the stunningly beautiful wording of the King James, *God so **loved** the world, that he gave his only begotten Son, that whosoever believeth in him should not perish, but have everlasting life. For God sent not his Son into the world to condemn the world; but that the world through him might be saved.*[4]

Every person drawing breath on this terrestrial clay is *so loved* by God whether or not he or she ever believes. But John 14:21 suggests in a

---

4. *The Holy Bible: King James Version,* Electronic Edition of the 1900 Authorized Version., John 3:16–17 (Bellingham, WA: Logos Research Systems, Inc., 2009), emphasis mine.

way too high, too sacred, and too divine for finite minds to comprehend, that the heart of God reverberates with a rhythm of affection particular to those who love Him. The link in the John 14 segment to our concept of audacious love is found in the final sentence of verse 21. Of the one who loves Him and displays it by obedience, Jesus says, *I also will love him and will reveal Myself to him.*

   I . . . will show myself to them. (NIV)

   I . . . will manifest myself to him. (KJV)

   I . . . will disclose Myself to him. (NASB)

He kept His promise that glorious Sunday evening when all the disciples but Thomas were locked in a room, scared to death, on the third day after His crucifixion with rumors starting to circulate that His body was missing from the tomb. Suddenly, Jesus appeared in the room with them, raised from the dead, still bearing His scars, but very much alive.

He will reveal Himself like that to us, too, when we see Him face-to-face and all our tears get wiped away and our griefs somersault into joys. The promise that He would reveal Himself to those who loved Him had a startling literal interpretation for those original disciples. This side of heaven, you and I may not get to see revelations of His resurrected *Person* but we do indeed get to see revelations of His resurrection *power.* On occasions when He sees fit, we do get to experience such a thickness of His presence that, though we cannot see Him with our eyes, we know with all our hearts that He is there. Maybe the setting is corporate worship when the Spirit of God pours so powerfully upon us, we feel like if the scales would just fall from our eyes, there Christ would be, standing in our midst. Or maybe our pastor is bringing the kind of message Paul described in 1 Thessalonians 1:4–5 as he recalled the move of the Holy Spirit when they brought the gospel to Thessalonica.

For we know, brothers loved by God, that he has chosen you, because our gospel came to you not only in word, but also in power and in the Holy Spirit and with full conviction. (ESV)

For now, our physical eyes are too weak to behold the revelation of the resurrected Jesus but we can have the wide-open eyes Paul describes to the Ephesian believers.

I do not cease to give thanks for you, remembering you in my prayers, that the God of our Lord Jesus Christ, the Father of glory, may give you the Spirit of wisdom and of revelation in the knowledge of him, having the eyes of your hearts enlightened, that you may know what is the hope to which he has called you, what are the riches of his glorious inheritance in the saints, and what is the immeasurable greatness of his power toward us who believe, according to the working of his great might that he worked in Christ when he raised him from the dead and seated him at his right hand in the heavenly places.[5]
(Eph. 1:16–20)

Take that in one more time: *the Spirit of wisdom and revelation in the knowledge of him, having the eyes of your hearts enlightened.* This, my friend, is the ultimate experience until the day we see His face: heart glimpses and spiritual senses that Jesus is near.

That He is at work. That we, too, get to work with Him.[6]

That He surrounds us. Meets with us. Abides in us. Abounds with love for us.

---

5. ESV.
6. Mark 16:20; 2 Cor. 6:1

That His Spirit dwelling within us is filling every cavern and reaching every limb.

We walk by faith and not by sight.[7] Sight alone physically sees but faith, bless God, perceives. And this, my patient fellow sojourner, is my favorite part of audacious love:

The pure enjoyment of Jesus' presence.

He's always there whether or not we ever perceive Him but nothing in this human experience is like an uncommon, sacred moment when, for the briefest flash of time, the veil seems thin. We are called to faithfulness no matter what and no matter how long it's been since we really felt His presence but we are well authorized by that very portion of Ephesians 1 to ask God to grant us the Spirit of wisdom and revelation and to grace us with hearts enlightened to see what mortal eyes cannot. The sights our hearts might behold are as boundless as Christ's imagination but they can occur any time He makes Himself known with unusual presence, power, passion, or partnership. Say, for instance,

Participating with Him in something that is humanly impossible or naturally unexplainable. Knowing full-well that He just enabled you to do something you were utterly incapable of doing.

Being surprised by Him. Slack-jawed over something He's done.

---

7. 2 Cor. 5:7

Awakening to the realization in the middle of an action that you've been sent by Him on a mission of sorts. Or, sometimes more astonishingly that He, the sovereign Son of God, just sent someone on a mission to you.

Getting a text from somebody saying, "I couldn't quit praying for you this morning. I feel like God really wants to remind you that He is with you and that He loves you so much." Nobody had seen your angst that morning but God. Nobody but He heard you wail. The Creator of the Universe literally appointed someone through the leadership of His Holy Spirit within them to reach out to you in His Name. How's that for audacious love? Never take that lightly.

Experiencing an unusually strong sense of Him in prayer, on a walk, on a drive. In the middle of a crisis or in an accident. In the despair of our unrelenting loneliness.

In His great mercy, we might sense His hand wrapped tightly around us even in our darkest sin.[8]

Seeing startling providence in what others call coincidence: *that* can be divine revelation. Being led by Him. Filled by Him. Fed by Him through His Word.

I've knelt before Jesus in absolute weakness—demoralized by circumstance, stress, sickness, spiritual attack, or harsh criticism—drained of every drop of energy, and, instead of standing up in faith like I'd usually do, counting on the strength to come, I've on occasion sensed His strength well up within me that very moment. Maybe that's not big enough to qualify as a manifestation of Christ to everybody but, to me,

---

8. Ps. 139:10

shifting from human weakness to supernatural strength in the length of a single breath is a miracle.

Jesus has never appeared to me. I've never heard His audible voice. But He has revealed Himself and His audacious love to me in countless ways. I have been moved by His Word at times so strongly that I've put my face in my hands and wept, or gotten out of my chair and gone face-down to the floor, or felt so energized and alive I had to come straight to my feet and pace the floor. Sometimes I purely have to slap my desk over the beauty and power of the Scriptures. That's not natural. That's the Spirit of Truth within the heart of a believer bearing witness to the Word of Truth in that pair of hands. It's not of our own doing. It's God. That's precisely the wonder of it. Personalities differ dramatically. You may not be as demonstrative and you're not as prone to slap your desk but, if you've walked with Jesus very long, I bet you know what it's like to feel extraordinarily moved by His Word in a way you know is His Spirit and not just emotion. The difference between adrenaline and anointing is in the fruit. If the results are eternal, that's anointing.

Sometimes the Holy Spirit will well up inside of me with enough force that I have to stop what I'm doing and completely change plans to follow the leadership of His Spirit *as best as I know how.* Those last six words are important. I'm a flawed woman with limited understanding trying to follow a flawless Savior with an infinite mind. Sometimes that welling up of Christ's Spirit seems to come with inaudible but discernible directions. I've contacted people I haven't talked to in ages only to find them—that very moment—desperate for encouragement or help or prayer. If you've been at this long, I bet you have, too. I have on occasion been compelled by the Holy Spirit to sit down by a total stranger in an airport, strike up a conversation with her, and soon find myself in an encounter so divinely orchestrated that only faithlessness could call it a coincidence. I've been in the full stride of a Bible lesson at an event and, without even thinking it through, stopped right in front of a person in the audience as I made the next point and learned later how specific it was to her. I end up as slack-jawed as she. Only an all-knowing, audaciously loving Savior reveals Himself that personally, intricately, and mercifully.

Those kinds of things are not my everyday experiences but neither are they isolated rarities. Many believers from diverse denominations, backgrounds, regions, countries, and traditions could testify to moments when Christ seems to reveal Himself, His power or His abounding affection in an extraordinary fashion. Like me, they believe moments like these can be valid experiences with Christ through His Spirit because Scripture blatantly says they can be. I'm not looking for something beyond what the Bible affirms, but I want every single thing within that Book that pleases Jesus to give me. He has denied my requests multiple times but every divine *yes* puts steel in my bones to keep seeking, asking, and knocking. I think that's how He likes it. He is perfectly capable of saying no, but God forbid that we fail to receive because we refuse to ask (James 4:2).

Moses had the audacity to ask God to show him His glory and God didn't strike him dead, give him leprosy, or turn him into a pillar of salt.[9] Moses didn't get to see God's face but he got the awe-striking, jaw-dropping privilege of being covered by His very hand in the cleft of the rock as His glory passed by. The chapter closes astoundingly with Moses seeing the back of God.[10] I think that's the way it is sometimes, figuratively speaking. We don't know it was God until the event passes by and we "see His back," but let there be no doubt: seeing God's back is enough to get us out of the black. You and I may ask for a gaze and only

9. Exod. 33:18
10. Exod. 33:23

get a glimpse, but the intriguing question on the table is this: would we have gotten the glimpse without asking for the gaze?

The Word of God is the only concrete for a pair of mortal feet.

It is God-breathed.

Unmatched.

Absolutely authoritative and utterly holy.

It is bread and meat.

It is light to our eyes and honey to our lips.[11]

It is water[12] and it is fire.[13] The Bible has thrilled me, stilled me, drilled me, filled me, and nearly killed me for thirty solid years. The Son of God saved my soul and the Word of God saved my mind. Those pages are the most sacred treasures fingertips of flesh can brush. We cannot hold Jesus with our human hands but we catch clutch our Bibles to our chests and cry out with all our might.

Those pages reveal to us in permanent ink a God who is willing to be encountered and known and experienced and moved by mortals. To subtract the miraculous from God is to deny that He is who He says He is. To say that He no longer performs wonders is to claim that He is no longer wonderful. To say that He can no longer speak to us through His Spirit in our inner man is to say that He—immortal, invisible, *and immutable*—has dramatically changed. God didn't call us to control the Spirit. He called us to be controlled *by* the Spirit. We don't get nervous and throw out the Spirit. We go to the trouble to test the Spirit.[14]

Scripture is complete. It cannot be added to or subtracted from. It is the Truth by which every other notion must be measured. But, within those very Scriptures we discover the Spirit of God who speaks. He

---

11. Ps. 19:10
12. Eph. 5:26
13. Jer. 23:29
14. 1 Thess. 5:19–21; 1 John 4:1

teaches, convicts, reminds, appoints, sanctifies, gifts, anoints. *He leads.*[15] Right there in those pages we meet the One who can cause a donkey to speak, a sun to stand still, a desert to bloom, a river to part, a rock to gush water, a raven to feed a prophet, an axe head to float, a fish to swallow a man, a fish to spit out a man, a fish to pay taxes, a few fish to feed thousands (He appears to like fish), a hand to appear out of nowhere and write on a wall, a head and hands to topple off an idol, rains to start, rains to stop, barren wombs to conceive, and, one glorious day when He has full sway, He'll cause trees of the fields to clap their hands.

Until then, we are wise women indeed to throw our hands over our mouths before we're quick to say what God doesn't still do. Let's shove our faith into the hands of a God who can do anything.

> *"Look, I am Yahweh, the God of all flesh.*
> *Is anything too difficult for Me?"* (Jer. 32:27)

Here's the thing. We are about to go our separate directions and set off on our own future adventures with Jesus. I can't tell you exactly what yours will look like or precisely what to expect. You couldn't do that for me either. Galatians 5:18 says that we are led by the Spirit, not by the law. Let's admit it. Laws would at least be a lot easier to identify even if they're a lot less fun. Legalism is not nearly as risky, but you and I aren't called to legalistic righteousness. We are called to live by the Spirit and Galatians 5:25 says *since we live by the Spirit, we must also follow the Spirit.* Following the Spirit requires getting into the Scriptures because we can know for certain the Spirit will never lead us contrary to His Word.

---

15. Acts 10:19; 11:12; 13:2; 16:6; 16:7

Following the Spirit also takes discernment. Insight. Perception. And, since we are human, that means most of us who take the risk of being led by the Spirit rather than a list of laws will get it wrong sometimes.

We'll probably look foolish sometimes.

Have to say we blew it sometimes.

But I will say this without a single hesitation: I would rather err trying to obey God than play it safe and quench His Spirit. He looks at our hearts. Our motives. He searches out our thought processes and recognizes the twists and turns of our understanding. Tuck this verse into your shirt pocket on the path of your adventures as a servant of Christ. Keep it handy when you feel judged or feel like judging.

Who are you to pass judgment on the servant of another?
It is before his own master that he stands or falls.
And he will be upheld, for the Lord is able to make him stand.
(Rom. 14:4 ESV)

It takes some audacity to put yourself out there and live by the Spirit. After all, what if you misunderstand? What if you're wrong? What if, one morning, you feel unusually burdened for a neighbor and believe that the Holy Spirit is leading you to drop by her house on the way to work and pray for her and, come to think of it, perhaps He might even be directing you to bake her a pound cake? Then, what if you—full of faith and anticipation—drop by her house and it turns out she doesn't need prayer, she can't eat sugar, and she's annoyed to no end? What then?

Three words: eat pound cake.

Right there in the driveway. Without a knife and fork or napkin. Just pick the thing up and bite right into it. It will make you feel better. And it might make God smile and I bet anything He'll bless you for trying to believe Him and trying to bless her and, a few days later, you might even manage to laugh.

If our heart's desire is to show people the love of Christ and do them good, then most of the time we'll do little harm even if it turns out we misunderstood. If, for whatever reason, we do accidentally cause harm, we take responsibility for it, ask forgiveness, and seek God's help to correct it. If what we think the Holy Spirit is leading us to do could be met with opposition or insult, we better fly like the wind to some mature people in the faith for counsel before we take a single step. If they tell us, based solidly on Scripture, that we've most likely misunderstood, we are tremendously wise to stand down. We'll maximize the joy and minimize the bewilderment if we realize from the onset that, in matters that aren't black and white, we're occasionally bound to get some wrong.

On Easter Sunday just a few weeks ago as I write this, my son-in-law, Curtis, preached a high-voltage sermon on the resurrection of Christ, then invited all of us in the congregation who knew Christ personally to come forward to take communion. At our church, five or six couples, depending on the crowd, are designated to stand in front, each holding a set of the elements. Those wishing to receive can choose any line and, when it is your turn, one spouse will offer you the bread and say, "*the body of Christ broken for you,*" and the other will offer you the cup to dip it in and say, "*the blood of Christ poured out for you.*" It's so personal and powerful, so face-to-face, that I nearly bawl every time.

Our church was packed that Sunday for Easter services so the lines for taking the elements were unusually long. After the song had gone on for some time, I started craning my neck to spy the hold up and couldn't understand for the life of me why one of the couples had only a few sporadic takers and all the other couples had droves lined up to receive. *How rude*, I thought. The forsaken couple was the furthest to the left so I reasoned, then again, that perhaps most people simply could not see them. When it was time for our row to go forward, I was bound by duty and spiritual maturity to save that precious couple from further slight. I made a beeline straight to the two of them to receive communion and, as always, was moved by the tenderness of the words. One beautiful thing about being active in a local body of believers is that, on occasion, someone calls you by name.

"*Miss Beth,*" the wife said holding the bread, "*the body of Christ broken for you.*"

I received it.

"*Miss Beth,*" the husband said holding the cup, "*the blood of Christ poured out for you.*"

I received it.

I returned to my seat and something wondrous happened. The bite of bread in my mouth that I'd dipped in the cup got bigger and bigger. It got so big, in fact, that I couldn't seem to swallow it. I didn't know exactly what was happening but I'd been taking communion for forty years. I was undoubtedly experiencing a fresh work. Whatever was occurring in my mouth was an altogether different sensation than I'd ever taken away from the Lord's Table. *Perhaps*, I thought to myself, *it is because this is most assuredly Christ's favorite anniversary to celebrate.* A day can't get better than getting raised from the dead. I supposed the Holy Spirit was blessing the elements to an extraordinary measure. The more I thought about it, the fuller my cheeks got. It was like the bread was multiplying in my mouth, like a personal miracle of loaves and fishes. I dared not look to my right or my left but I hoped against hope that this wonderment was happening to the whole congregation.

I worked the elements around in my mouth, wondering what manner of significance it had that I could barely swallow it. I kept my lips pressed together for fear of a leak but moved my jaw up and down and side to side to see what would happen. I'd confessed my sins silently before I'd gone up to receive so surely this was not a punishment. *So*, I was left to reason, *what could this phenomenon be but a blessing?* This tender *why-me* ushered tears to my eyes. After all these years of communion, what an unusual, expected thing had happened to me. Perhaps God had looked favorably upon me for preferring a couple that many in our congregation had shunned. I planned to tell no one but to ponder deeply within my heart how God had multiplied the bread within my very mouth.

An hour and a half later, four generations of us Moores were at my dining room table eating roast beef, mashed potatoes, gravy, sweet potatoes, green beans, yeast rolls, and other Southern goodnesses stirred up by my own spoon. We talked about how anointed the sermon had been and marveled over the crowds and boasted in the Lord for sustaining Curtis to preach four services straight with such power and grace. It had been a glorious Resurrection Sunday morning. We talked about how handsome Jackson, my grandson, looked in his suit and tie and how much we loved his little sister Annabeth's brand new Easter dress. We talked about how wonderful the worship was and our deep hopes and prayers that some of our guests had given their hearts to Jesus.

My youngest daughter, Melissa, loves liturgy in a worship service as much as anyone you'll ever meet so it was no surprise when she brought up how thankful she was that we'd observed communion that day. I kept my secret manifestation to myself but did indeed offer this ponderance for table conversation:

"I wonder why so few people went to the couple on the extreme left. After all, it would have taken some of the length off the other lines. I felt a little bad for them. What was that about? Are they new?"

Amanda and Melissa looked at me oddly and so, I noticed, did Curtis. I kept shaking salt on my green beans to purposely let the question hang in the air and leave room for the conviction of the Holy Spirit. Clearly no one had the maturity at the table to notice the oversight at church but me. After several seconds Curtis said,

"Ma'am, are you talking about the couple offering the gluten-free?"

"Come again?" I asked, needing a little clarity and thinking I might have over-salted the beans.

"Yeah," he said, *"when I told the congregation to come forward, I told them that the gluten-free elements were at that end if they had special dietary needs."*

Definitely I'd over salted the greens. I shifted them around on my plate until they were sufficiently whitewashed by the mashed potatoes then mumbled,

"Oh."

I wondered how I'd missed that but then recalled being a little distracted right then by Annabeth's darling new headband with a bow so big and heavy that it wouldn't stay on her head.

"Mom," Amanda leaned forward, nosing into my business. *"Did you take the gluten-free elements?"*

It looked like to me that Memmaw could use some more tea so I stood up to fetch it.

"Mom?" Amanda pressed again, this time a little louder.

With this, Melissa set her fork down, realizing by now that underway was a family moment not to be missed for all the roast gravy in the universe. Then she started in with it. *"Mom?"*

I sat back down, returned my napkin to my lap and muttered, "*Maybe.*"

You could have heard four generations of Moores and Joneses howl their heads off for ten country miles. As it turned out, the supernatural manifestation in my mouth was nothing but the gluten-free. Thank goodness the elements themselves, blessed and broken and poured out, were not without effect. This kind of unfortunate mishap could have been avoided if we still had church bulletins. A church could put an Arkansas girl raised on cornbread, biscuits, sorghum molasses, and grits into shock with gluten free bread. I don't know that I shouldn't wear a medic alert bracelet from now on to church. No wonder that loaf didn't tear right. When I told my family how moved I'd been as that bite of bread in my mouth grew bigger and bigger, we laughed till the tears squirted out of our eyes. Don't try to tell me Jesus didn't think it was funny.

All said, I'm still going to put myself out there and take the chance of experiencing something supernatural and primarily because of Kendra. One Saturday morning several months ago, Keith was out of town so I got to sleep a little later than usual, then bask in a good, long time with Jesus. I'd told God a few days earlier that I was so ready for some good jaw-dropping divine encounters because it had been too long since I'd had one. That particular Saturday morning I hadn't thought much about it. His Word had leapt off the page, captured my imagination, and spun my mind with wonder. I finished up my prayer time, closed my Bible and hooked my blue pen on the spiral of my journal. I picked up my empty coffee cup and walked around the kitchen island to the dishwasher. In those few moments, I had the most random thought. Out of the blue, a particular Metro bus stop in Houston circled through my memory like a cul-de-sac and stopped. I'd never ridden that bus or stopped at that bench and its location was nowhere near my home or work. Numerous Metro bus stops were closer. The specifics were so unsolicited and peculiar that they gave me pause. Had I not just been in Bible study and prayer, I probably wouldn't have given it a second thought but the timing after an unrushed morning with Jesus made me suspect something was up.

Literally *up*.

I heard no words. I saw no visions. But somehow in a way hard to adequately explain, I believed it was very possibly the leadership of the Holy Spirit. I also somehow knew in that moment to take some money. I got dressed, went by the ATM, and headed half an hour from my home to that exact bus stop on the feeder road of I-10. I knew I could get there and discover that I'd inadvertently imagined the whole thing but, honestly, what did I have to lose but a little money and a tad of dignity? I drove through an adjacent parking lot and pulled up as close behind the bus stop as I could. Not a soul was there, but I put my car in park and unzipped my purse to get the cash ready anyway. As I live and breathe, in the moment it took to get out the money, a woman walked up to the stop to catch the bus. My heart jumped into my throat and every butterfly in Texas flew into my stomach. Not knowing the bus schedule, I was too afraid to pause so I jumped out of the car, not wanting to miss my opportunity, and headed her way.

> *"Please forgive me for being forward. I so very much don't want to scare you but I really do believe Jesus has sent me to this very stop to give you this."*

I took her hand and stuck the layers of folded-up cash in her palm and pressed her fingers over it. She was taken aback as anyone would have been whether or not God were involved. As her eyes grew as wide as saucers, I tried to figure out whether her shock was positive or negative. A person could get a concussion from the size purse she had hanging from her shoulder. I told her that Jesus loved her and cared deeply about what she was going through then I walked back toward my car.

"Ma'am!" She yelled.

I turned around.

"I know why He sent you!"

I responded, *"You do?"*

"I know He's been telling me to move out of a bad situation. I looked into moving and, no matter where I looked, every apartment complex needed a deposit. I told Him if I had the money for a deposit, I'd move."

I smiled, relief washing over me like somebody was spraying me down with a water hose. *"Well, then,"* I said. *"I suppose you better start packing up."*

She was beside herself. I was beside myself, too. I grinned and said good-bye, got in my car, and put it in reverse. Before I could touch the gas pedal, she ran over to my window and I rolled it down.

"Can I hug you?" she asked.

I can hardly keep from crying as I recount this simple scene to you. *"You sure can,"* I answered. I put my car back in park, climbed out of it, and we hugged each other purple. We didn't say much. We just hugged like two women who'd been left red-faced by the audacious love of Jesus. When I drove away, I yelled at the top of my lungs, *"Wooooohooooo!!!!"* I couldn't help myself. I shouted *"hallelujah"* and beat the steering wheel with the palm of my hand. Then I screamed, *"That was so much fun!"*

You couldn't swear by me that my tires hit the pavement all the way home. Somebody will insist that I was delusional, that God doesn't lead these days like that, and that, of course, the woman took the money whether those were her circumstances or not. *After all*, someone will say, *what fool wouldn't?* And that's okay with me. I'll take that chance on the mere possibility of a holy nod from God. Let me err on the side of faith. That Kendra-kind of moment hasn't happened to me very often but, when it has, it has been so utterly thrilling I could hardly catch my breath.

The Holy Spirit worked wildly in the early New Testament church, leading and compelling and stopping and redirecting and empowering followers of Jesus in brow-raising ways. In Acts 16:6–10, the Holy Spirit forbid Paul, Timothy, and Silas from going one direction where they sought to preach and, when they turned another direction, He stopped them again. Then Paul had a vision in the night.

> *A Macedonian man was standing and pleading with him, "Cross over to Macedonia and help us!" After he had seen the vision, we immediately made efforts to set out for Macedonia, concluding that God had called us to evangelize them.* (Acts 16:9–10)

Concluding that God had called us. Sometimes when something is not written in concrete but it's not contradictory to Scripture, we might have to risk drawing a conclusion. We tread carefully, yes, but we can't just sit in neutral forever.

Oh, but we can go one wilder than that. Take a look at this event in Acts 8:26–40.

> *[26] An angel of the Lord spoke to Philip: "Get up and go south to the road that goes down from Jerusalem to Gaza." (This is the desert road.) [27] So he got up and went. There was an Ethiopian man, a eunuch and high official of Candace, queen of the Ethiopians, who*

was in charge of her entire treasury. He had come to worship in Jerusalem ²⁸*and was sitting in his chariot on his way home, reading the prophet Isaiah aloud.*

²⁹*The Spirit told Philip, "Go and join that chariot."*

³⁰*When Philip ran up to it, he heard him reading the prophet Isaiah, and said, "Do you understand what you're reading?"*

³¹*"How can I," he said, "unless someone guides me?" So he invited Philip to come up and sit with him.* ³²*Now the Scripture passage he was reading was this:*

He was led like a sheep to the slaughter,

and as a lamb is silent before its shearer,

so He does not open His mouth.

³³*In His humiliation justice was denied Him.*

Who will describe His generation?

For His life is taken from the earth.

³⁴*The eunuch replied to Philip, "I ask you, who is the prophet saying this about—himself or another person?"* ³⁵*So Philip proceeded to tell him the good news about Jesus, beginning from that Scripture.*

³⁶*As they were traveling down the road, they came to some water. The eunuch said, "Look, there's water! What would keep me from being baptized?" [*³⁷*And Philip said, "If you believe with all your heart you may." And he replied, "I believe that Jesus Christ is the Son of God."]* ³⁸*Then he ordered the chariot to stop, and both Philip and the eunuch went down into the water, and he baptized him.* ³⁹*When they came up out of the water, the Spirit of the Lord carried Philip away, and the eunuch did not see him any longer. But he went on his way rejoicing.* ⁴⁰*Philip appeared in Azotus, and he was traveling and evangelizing all the towns until he came to Caesarea.*

Come on, now. That account gives a whole new meaning to getting carried away. If the Holy Spirit worked like that in the first generation of believers, is it not possible today in a world just as broken for Him to lead us to simply make a phone call? Or a visit? Or a trip across town to take a total stranger a little money? Listen, Jesus is worth wasting a pound cake. If we get it wrong trying to do someone right, I have a feeling God can sort it out.

If we stomp out every bit of spontaneity and edge out every inch of risk in our divine romance with Jesus, we are going to flatten what was meant to be the greatest thrill of our lives into the roadkill of religious routine. When you are head over heels in love, you make a fool of yourself sometimes. Paul put it this way: *If it seems we are crazy, it is to bring glory to God* (2 Cor. 5:13 NLT).

My friend, Kevin Perry, a fabulous family man, worship leader, and guitar player, recently sat back and listened with considerable glee to his two young daughters playing Barbies. He overheard the older one say to the younger, "She can't fly . . . but she can ride a horse in high heels." I don't know. Maybe you hate high heels. But I hope you don't hate being a woman because, make no mistake, a woman can do a lot of impressive things. Don't get all undone and distracted and down because you can't fly. That woman you see every morning in the mirror can still ride a horse in high heels like nobody's business. You've got this divine Groom in your life—this real, live infinitely greater Prince Charming, this One called Faithful and True—who really is going to burst through the sky someday on a white horse to save the day.[16] Until you see that white horse kicking up clouds of dust in the morning sky, you keep riding no matter how that bronco bucks. Dig in your heels and hang on for dear life. Pull those reins right when the Spirit says so then left when He switches it

---

16. Rev. 19:11

up. And, when Jesus does something spectacular, every now and then, just go ahead, throw caution to the wind, and hoot and holler your head off. You'll be surprised how much better you feel. Raise the bar on your praise and see what happens.

Enjoy Jesus. Have the wildest ride of your whole life with Him. He is the adventure. He's the best part. There in a bold and daring love for Him, we discover the life we were born for, our full-throttle gifting and anointing, our reason for existing, our soul-satisfaction, our full redemption, healthy human connection, countless answers to prayer, living words hopping off the sacred page onto our sidewalks and everything else of truest, purest value. To grant us these glorious consequences delights the heart of Christ. He is a Giver, after all, not a taker. But He Himself is the prize. I don't just mean that respectfully or maturely, smugly or theoretically. I'm not telling you that because I should. I mean that He really is.

The very best part.

My friend, Chris, told me a story recently that I can't get out of my head. When she was in her final year of college at the University of Sydney, she got to know a fellow student named Debra in her English Lit. class. She was the intimidating sort: an affluent, smart, socially gifted, party-queen swarmed by guys. As different as they were, Chris said, they'd drummed up a friendship and caught lunch together on campus quite often before class. When Debra didn't show up for several days, Chris was concerned but, with no contact information, all she could do was wait it out. Three days into Debra's absence, Chris was in the university cafeteria working on an English paper over lunch when she heard a small commotion. She looked up to see Debra running toward her, nearly hyperventilating with excitement.

A bit taken aback, Chris asked her where she'd been and told her that she'd worried herself half to death. Here's what she said.

"I've been at a rave party and it was incredible. I have not slept for three days. We danced and danced and had so much fun. It was the best experience of my life. I have never felt so much love, I have never felt so much peace, I have never felt so much joy, and it was such an amazing experience I did not want you to miss out, so I saved you half."

She reached in her pocket then placed a substance in Chris's palm. It was Ecstasy. She didn't take it, but the irony of the exchange hit Chris in a way she said she'd never get over. Her friend, lost and frantically searching, was more anxious to share a synthetic drug on masquerade as love, peace, and joy, than a believer, found and saved to the uttermost, was anxious to share Jesus. She made up her mind that it would never happen again.

Jesus, the ecstatic joy of angels. The magnificent obsession of wide-eyed mortals delivered from hell and the grave.

When Chris told me that story, I was already writing this book. I've thought about it every day, supposing that's what I'm trying to do here in these pages. I have no idea how effective this will ever be or what it will mean to a single soul. I'm a bit of a train wreck. But, one way or the other, here's me running across the cafeteria. Considering the source, I'll probably trip over somebody's purse, knock down six people carrying loaded cafeteria trays, slip on lime Jell-O and slide under a table of seminary professors and land in the splits. And I'll think I should have worn leotards and leg warmers. I'll, then, probably need a minute to recover because it's been a long time since I've done the splits. But I'll get back up and start running again. And I'll be the one hollering. Since I may not know your name, kindly consider the heart behind me screaming, *Hey, you!* Forgive the stares. People in public places can't help being nosy.

Here's me, now, standing at your table, digging in my pocket and trying to place in your palm the only thing in all of life that has ever really worked for me.

Jesus is Savior to me and He is Lord. He is Master, Author, and Finisher. He is Deliverer and Redeemer. He is holy, wise, all-knowing, and all-powerful. But He is also the biggest blast in my life. And, forgive me for saying so, but that's no small claim. I'm sanguine to the bone. Fun is important to me. I know a blast when I'm having one.

So, anyway, here you go. And here's the best part. We don't have to half Him. Have all of Him. Enjoy every glorious ounce of Him. He's all yours. Have the audacity to take Him up on everything He is. And, if you do, I dare you not to live an adventure. And I'll be wishing I could sit at your funeral one day and see the officiant pull out the program with your picture on it and say to the congregation, "*You see that woman right there?*"

"*Uh-huh,*" we'll all respond.

Then he'll draw a deep breath and say at full volume,

She had verve.

And, yep, I'll be absolutely certain, without a shadow of a doubt, that he rolled his r's.